CW00496403

Derrick de Kerckhove

The Architecture of Intelligence

Birkhäuser – Publishers for Architecture
Basel • Boston • Berlin

A CIP catalogue record for this book is available from the Library of Congress, Washington D.C., USA.

Deutsche Bibliothek Cataloging-in-Publication Data

Kerckhove, Derrick /de:
The architecture of intelligence / Derrick de Kerckhove. - Basel ; Boston ; Berlin : Birkhäuser, 2001
(The IT revolution in architecture)
ISBN 3-7643-6451-3

Original edition:
L'architettura dell'intelligenza (Universale di Architettura 98, collana fondata da Bruno Zevi; La Rivoluzione Informatica, sezione a cura di Antonino Saggio).

Printed on acid-free paper produced of chlorine-free pulp. TCF ∞
Printed in Italy
ISBN 3-7643-6451-3

9 8 7 6 5 4 3 2 1 http://www.birkhauser.ch

Contents

For Eckart Wintzen,
a superior architect of intelligence

When Antonino Saggio asked me for a contribution to the "IT Revolution in Architecture" series, I was intrigued because that connection is clearly one of the most interesting bridges to draw between the real and the virtual. However, because I had no expertise in either architecture or web design, I decided to take the project on as an experiment in "connected intelligence".

I want to thank first my stellar research assistants, Ana Viseu, who is doing research about identity on line at the University of Toronto, and Maria-Luisa Palumbo, who published the previous book in the same collection and spent the summer and more surfing the web. She is the translator of this book in Italian and the author of the appendix. During the summer, Tina Lasala, a Junior Fellow at the McLuhan Program, spent many hours in front of a screen for this book and so did Patrizia Schettino.

I had a lot of help and expertise available to me thanks to a group of young architects, designers and engineers from the Toronto area under the name of "RNA connective". Many members, among whom Tonik Wojtyra, Chris Hardwicke and Glenn Mann contributed their insights during our weekly meetings. But I want to make a special mention of those members of the connective who took on special responsibilities. First, there is Marc Ngui who ran the meetings and whose truly personal and highly original contribution can be found in all the drawings which tell the stories of our relationships with technology. Arnold Wu, I thank for his brilliant illustrations and for directing most of the graphic contents of the book. Peter Marshall did the cover and many stunning images of painted collages that appear from place to place. Tonik Wojtyra's contribution is found in the stretched series of images in the first chapter. I want to thank Maurice Benayoun and Z-A productions, Joachim Sauter and Art + Com in Berlin, Char Davies and Immersence, Rafael Lozano-Hemmer, Jan Willem van Kuilenburg and Monolab for the permission to use images from their many exceptional projects. Harry Hampel supplied us with his moving pictures of Berlin with and without The Wall.

The book is posted on *Openflows*, a website specializing in collaborative text filtering and in what its developers, Felix Stalder and Jesse Hirsh, call "open source intelligence". This site is moderated and open to everybody. Its purpose is to refine information to its highest level of pertinence by connecting the different areas of expertise of the readers/contributors. To connect with this site, go to *www.openflows.org.*

DERRICK DE KERCKHOVE
Nice, March 26, 2001

Ddek

preface by Antonino Saggio

This book is a treasure trove of intuitions, links, paths. The reader will quickly note that there is more to it than merely a large quantity of data. Rather it is the quality itself of the information that is high since the ideas arrive filtered through one of the centers that brings together many threads in the new web system. We are speaking here of the McLuhan Program in Culture and Technology at the University of Toronto and its director Derrick de Kerckhove who carries out philosophical, scientific and technological thought on the wave of the information technology revolution.
The fact that de Kerckhove and the authors who have written for this series met at a symposium (the physical location was Zurich and the date was 12 April 2000) is significant. Architectural culture needs qualified and open traveling companions. We architects welcome the thinker de Kerckhove, the first non-architect in the series. If our way of thinking, a way of thinking completely applied to construction, can also give something to other disciplines, then why not?
But the fact that this book is a treasure trove of ideas represents only one aspect and not even the most important one at that. What is decisive here is that this book places us in a profoundly critical position.
This involves, from time to time, measuring one's own technological, as well as sociological or philosophical, know-how against that which Derrick proposes here. (We will call him, in the American style, only by his first name or instead by the acronym Ddek, omitting the list of prestigious titles and the even more numerous series of translations of his works into many languages. In Italy alone we should recall the book from 1995, *La civilizzazione videocristiana* for Feltrinelli or subsequent ones for Mondadori and Costa & Nolan.)
So Ddek pushes us into a crisis on various levels. Imagine that strong but timid student in Florence who "desperately" wants to organize a conference dedicated to Zevi and does not even have e-mail. And I see my oldest colleague who has never navigated on the Internet. But continually new adolescences, new puberties must be faced and the great efforts of the past and promise of the new must never be forgotten. I understand those who have already conquered much but who have never thought… perhaps… about what Linux means as a new way of working, or the freedom of interconnected communities or even the relationship between the mental world (the "theater" of our imagination) and the virtual space of the net. And, as if all this were not enough, one can explore between the lines of this book to follow those underground currents since, whenever an experience is recalled, there is always definitely something important behind it for deeper study.

Those who also participated in the process, one that saw the book devel-op from an initial invitation involving Maria Spina, through variou rebounds, modifications and leaps forward, may be pushed even furthe into a crisis. In my case, there were two reasons. The first regards th method. Ddek did something that was apparently simple but incredibl for an author: he put this book on-line while he was working on it. Makin a book public while it is being written shrugs off many customs, jeal-ousies, limitations and fears. This is a lesson to be considered again an again: on the other hand, he has already written it down in one of his prin-ciples. In the great world of the net, the only way to be acknowledged is t do something useful for everyone and Derrick has connected intelligenc and individuals around him.

The second aspect is content. Anyone who thinks simultaneously of th past and future, as if the world of ideas crosses moments in history to fin itself each time in front of our eyes, can only be struck by his masterf reflections on Vitruvius and the Alphabet.

Today, the need for creating a new alphabet is pressing and exactly wh *The Architecture of Intelligence* has begun to construct. A space that st does not yet completely exist but one we can begin to intuit and, throug the principles illustrated here, can begin to shape.

Consider the wonderful metaphor of fish he offers us. Fish know only th fluid that, just like air, surrounds them. They know nothing either of wh the sea or lake or river really is and know even less about the space which we humans live. Only a jump beyond that aquatic surface can ope up the sensation of another space that definitely exists, even if it is neith frequented nor understood.

Throughout history we have lived in different spaces and architects, usir different alphabets, have given them form: informal space, gestural ar primitive, pre-Miletus (or pre-alphabet as Ddek calls it); the space arte alized by the Greeks and Romans; the sacred and mystic space befo Giotto; that perspective space of the Renaissance; the industrial ar mechanical, analytical and non-perspective space after Cézanne. Eac new space on arriving has required new principles and new alphabe that have been created through difficult, exhausting, rough but excitir processes. Regarding the new information space that de Kerckhove ca Cyber (the battle for the name is however still open), we can only beg to catch a glimpse of a few characteristics. Like dolphins that take in ox gen to jump from the sea and follow ships and see the outlines of islan and coasts, a few pioneers are working in an attempt to define the pos bilities and principles of precisely this new space. This book will help y join in this search.

www.arc.uniroma1.it/sagg

1. The Invention(s) of Space

1. Spatialization

We are witnessing here the birth of a new domain, a new space that simply did not exist before (Margaret Wertheim, 1999).

The architecture of intelligence is the architecture of connectivity. It is the architecture that brings together the three main spatial environments that we live in and with today: mind, world and networks. *With the exponential force of its own big bang, cyberspace is exploding into being before our very eyes. Just as cosmologists tell us that the physical space of our universe burst into being out of nothing some fifteen billion years ago, so also the ontology of cyberspace is ex nihilo*[1].

The appearance of cyberspace which is supported by the Internet and the World Wide Web invites us to reconsider the previous two kinds of space we had become accustomed to.

> Hippodamus, of Miletus, a Greek architect of the 5th century B.C. It was he who introduced order and regularity into the planning of cities, in place of the previous intricacy and confusion. For Pericles he planned the arrangement of the harbor-town Peiraeus at Athens. When the Athenians founded Thurii in Italy he accompanied the colony as architect, and afterwards, in 408 B.C., he superintended the building of the new city of Rhodes. His schemes consisted of series of broad, straight streets, cutting one another at right angles. (*Encyclopedia Britannica*, 11th edition, 1910)

City grids
Hippodamos of Miletus was the first in the history of the West to introduce what would become the standard city grid that is characteristic of North America, the only country in Western civilization that was until recently entirely and exclusively predicated on the phonetic alphabet. Until Hippodamos, towns grew without a plan, as per was needed for housing, defense and prayer. Hippodamos introduced a principle of rationality – a principle which translates into "proportionality" when applied to architecture – that was reflected in every aspect of Roman life until the fall of the Roman Empire. Later, the printing press reinforced space as we know it to structure cultural and social consciousness.

2. Proportion

The connection between the Greek alphabetic literacy and city grids is neither fortuitous nor accidental, but direct. The use of letters for the phonemes of human speech introduced a new relationship to space among the cultures that practised it. Instead of being an extension of the skin and an experience of the breathing lungs, space became an objective reality, subject to visual appreciation, analysis, theory, classification and management.

Why would the Greek alphabet have anything to do with space? Like the Internet today, the alphabet was – and remains – a core technology of human information-processing. Its use affects not only the contents of information, but also the structure of information-processing. Take perspective, for example. Why do people, first in Greece and Rome, and again after the invention of the press, develop a taste for perspective, symmetry, exact proportions and measurement in space, time and architecture as well as painting, music and scientific enquiry ? Furthermore, why didn't the Phoenicians who invented the first alphabet show any interest in perspective ?

What's the difference? By adding vowels to the line of consonants they already had borrowed from their Phoenician model, the Greeks made unambiguous the deciphering of the string of phonemes. You wouldn't need to know what the text was about to render it into a meaningful succession of words and sentences. Indeed, and this is the main clue to the difference in processing, the Greek scribes abandoned all the word separations that had been carefully maintained among the Phoenician scripts to distinguish the beginning and the end of words, sentences, paragraphs, etc. This implied a determinant change in the strategy of the brain to process the line of script, yielding the priority to analytical over contextual deciphering. It is eventually the new dominance of a principle of systematic analysis that resulted in the rightward relateralization of the reading direction in the Greco-Roman scripts.

3. Analysis

Perspective was nothing else than leaving out the movement in experience and having the image as residue. Pure recollection, and recollection only (Lars Spuybroek, 1998).

The optic chiasm

The same principle of analysis introduced the need for perspective both in physical and mental space. The appreciation of the comparative ratios of distance from the point of view to the objects of sight is something that satisfies not only the viewer, but also the viewer's brain. In fact, perspective very closely reflects the modality of information-processing that a literate brain adopts when it is invited to consider space. The need to align objects in space in terms of their proportionate relationships is an effect of the practice of reading and writing on how we make use of the optic chiasm.

The optic chiasm is the name given to the peculiar anatomy of vision that splits visual functions between the left and the right hemispheres of the brain. The vision of each eye is split vertically down the middle into two visual hemi-fields. The optic chiasm (from the Greek word chiasma for "cross-over") is based on the fact that the opposite sides of each hemisphere control the visual hemi-fields of both eyes, where most of vision is being processed. To be precise, the left hemi-fields of both the left and the right eyes are held in the occipital striate cortex at the back of the right hemisphere, and of course, the opposite region in the left hemisphere analyzes the right visual hemi-fields.

The probable reason why there is such a bizarre distribution of alternate hemi-fields, one going to the right and the next to the left hemisphere, is because there is an equally strange but acknowledged division of labor between the modalities of the two hemispheres. The right hemisphere "grabs" the vision (like a frame-grabber), while the left analyses it. This is for the eyes the equivalent of the functions of the hands: for the standard right-handed person, the left hand holds the bread, and the right hand cuts it. The overlap of the functions within the four visual hemi-fields guarantees that both functions are performed evenly over the whole available visual spectrum.

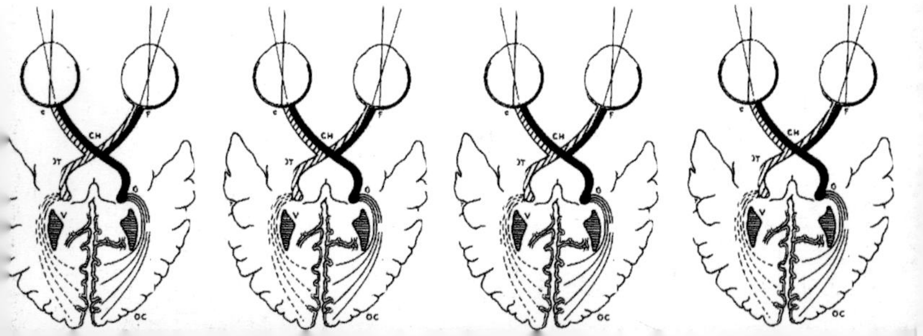

4. Perspective and Symmetry

The geometry of the mind is never a complete system (George Kelly, 1970).

Everything we see, according to neuroscientists, is the result n merely of the recording of the visual field by the brain, but also of cc stant calculation and calibration. A mind entrained by reading to ar lyze text could conceivably be encouraged to transport such analy cal skills to analyze space. The reading brain simply changes t basic equations of vision. Perspective is the result of the analysis space by time, which is distance. From the point of view of the subje looking at the world, the objects are represented/placed in propo tional relationships of distance. Foreshortening, a technique dev oped by the Greeks, is a way to reproduce the illusion of depth a distance on a two-dimensional plane.

The appreciation for symmetry and the calculation of perspecti would take full advantage of the horizontal parallax and the binocu vision provided by both eyes. Indeed, the slight difference of poir of-view coming from each eye would provide the brain with t means to instantly calculate ratios. That is why western people are "rational". And a mind encouraged to analyze space might also inclined to manage it and impose a rational grid on it when plann for it. We have to assume that Hippodamos was an avid reader.

Another avid reader, Marcus Vitruvius Pollio, produced the first treaty of architecture that has not been denied to us by the irrev ence of time. It was written under the reign of Augustus in Rome anc precious not only because it has provided the bedrock of princip and recipes for generations of architects from his time to our own (book is still required reading in many schools of architecture toda but also because it contains, at every chapter, a kind of compendi of what the preceding, now lost, texts of architecture, especia ancient Greek treatises of architecture, had to say. Vitruvius, in ot words equals continuity.

5. Firmitas – Utilitas – Venustas

Man looks at his world through transparent templates which he creates and then attempts to fit over the realities of which the world is composed (George Kelly, 1955).

The principles supported by Vitruvius reflect, as they should, the hidden structure of his literate mind and that of his clients and his followers for 2000 years. They are "Firmitas, Utilitas, Venustas", stability, utility, beauty. As the encyclopedia goes on to say:

> Of such principles or qualities the following appear to be the most important: size, harmony, proportion, symmetry, ornament and color. All other elements may be reduced under one or the other of these heads.

The visual bias of this array of principles should not be taken for granted, as it seems to have been by so many producers and consumers of architecture to this day. Buildings are presented as spectacles, not as places where comfort, communication, social interaction, health or other physiological considerations dominate. Beauty in Western art and architecture is an object of vision, all other senses being either ignored or serving as handmaidens. To be fair, Vitruvius does recommend at the outset that a good architect must also be acquainted with "grammar, music, painting, sculpture, medicine, geometry, mathematics and optics". He showed some interest in acoustics to the extent that it comes naturally into play in the building of theatres and basilicas and other official buildings in a culture where the human voice is not carried by electricity but by airwaves.

Vitruvius included many considerations about proportionality among the volumes and the geometry of structure, but the overall perception of the building is dominated by visualizing its façade. In other words, the building is quite literally a theory, something to look at, a theatrical construction. This visual bias puts the literate people in a perpetually frontal relationship with the world. This frontal relationship is a hidden principle of our literate past that is being challenged by the total surround quality of networks and Virtual Reality.

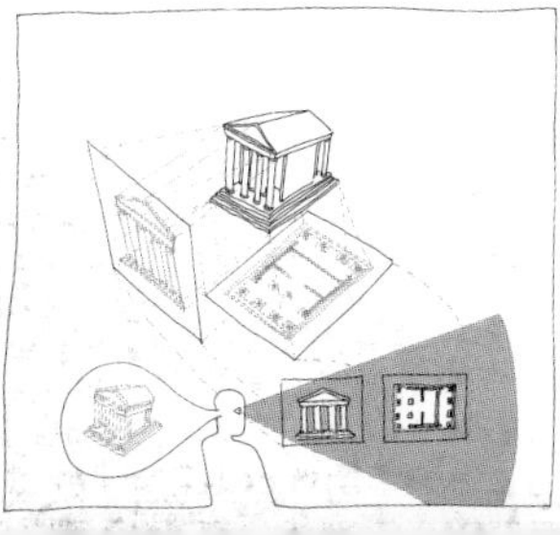

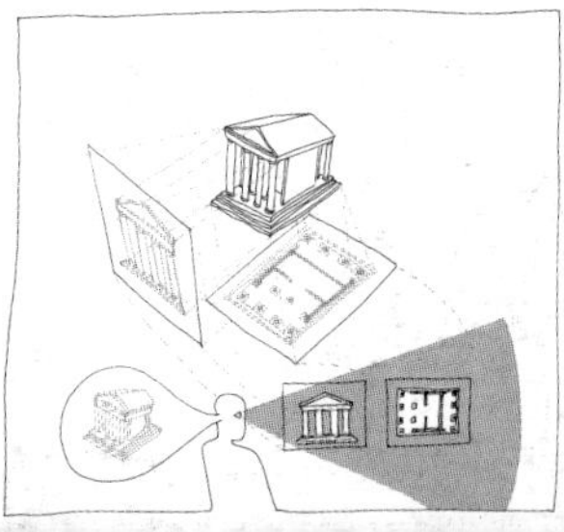

6. Representation

Space is a product of consciousness, and our perceived space is derived from a mix of direct and mediated stimulation (Peter Anders, 2000).

Mental space

The bias of representation comes mostly from the need for the mind to comprehend what the body is involved with. Through the bias of literacy, the bias of representation is reinforced and specialized because readers must translate text into images that the words represent.

The reason why the visual bias can dominate a fully literate culture is not only that most of the critical information going from the world to the mind will come through the portals of the eyes but also because reading requires the mind to develop the visualization process as "imagination". Literally, imagination is the power to create images in one's mind. This is what we do when we read. The interpretation of text demands that we exercise our imaginative skills constantly. But it also seems to require that we favor representation over direct knowledge or apprehension of things. Of course, the very notion of "direct knowledge" is quite absurd in the face of the evidence about how much the brain works just to get a coherent representation of what it takes for reality.
As John Frazer explains in a telescopic contraction of our knowledge of the brain:

> Our eyes transmit to our brains poor resolution, upside-down, mainly monochrome, moving two-dimensional images which the brain converts into a three-dimensional colored model which moves with us but is static relative to our eye movements. The brain censors out our obtrusive nose, fills in the gaps where the bundle of optic nerves leaving our eyes causes a blind spot, employs a rich repertory of tricks such as size constancy which prevents someone appearing to shrink as they move away, is easily deceived by false perspective and other illusions. Then the ultimate trick is played and the brain gives us the feeling that this virtual model in our brains is actually 'out there' and incorporates other information from the senses such as vibration in the air which it conveniently converts into sounds also "out there" (*The Architectural Relevance of Cyberspace*, in *Architects in Cyberspace*, Architectural Design Magazine, 1995, pp. 76-77).

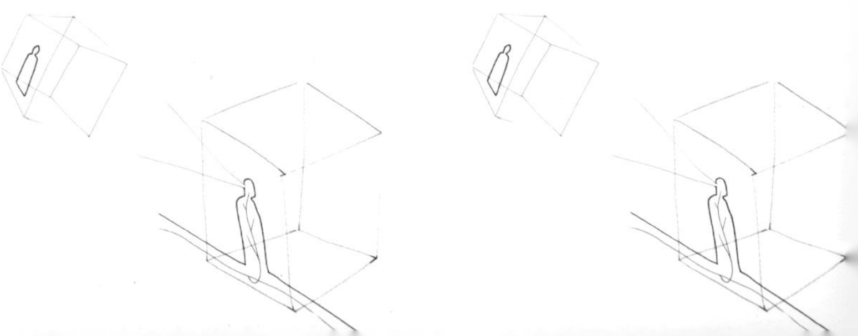

7. Internalization

A person anticipates events by construing their replications (George Kelly, 1955).

As readers, we learn to represent and internalize the visual field by repeating it in our imagination. It is because of this simple process that, quite literally, we "make up our mind". The mind finds a niche in individual heads. The mind of the western individual works by a kind of "inversion of perspective", not looking out, but looking in. In essence, the eye stands as the lens that both separates the inside from the outside in a clear focus and also inverts the axis of observation from the outwardly gaze directed at the world to the inwardly gaze directed at an internal theatre, a theoretical construct which we call the mind, believing that it is a private, silent, totally individualized universe devoted to imagination and thought. This is the "mental space" most of us are accustomed to, that we have developed since childhood and that we furnish with our daily experience, our memories and with our media. This intimate, internal space we have been taught to discipline since our earliest schooldays, and to tune finely with novels, poetry and theatre. We weave our own minds.

This mental space is thus a personalized mirror image of the physical space outside. It is, of course equally dependent on the alphabet. The fact is that readers of the alphabet got two spaces for the price of one: one inside their head, and the other, outside. The condition for the harmonious coexistence of both was and remains that the outside space be fixed and reliably pinned down by such rational disciplines as geography, geometry, architecture, cadastres, and that the inside space maintain a looser, but still determinative connection with rationality. That internal space still needs spatial and temporal coordinates, still expresses itself in terms of an internal frontal relationship between the "eye of the mind" and the internal object of its attention, and still rests upon a horizontal plane.

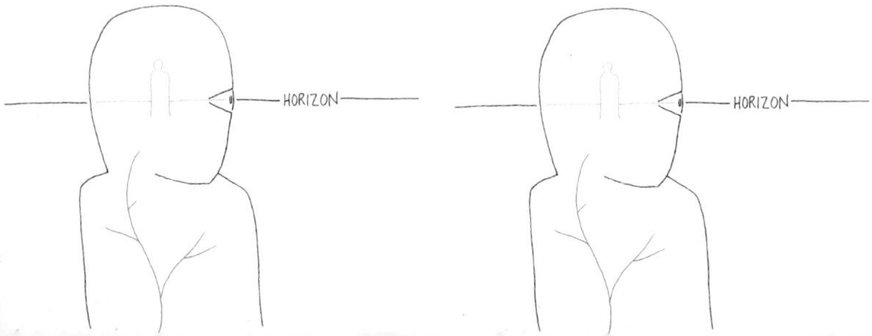

8. Objectivity

Our psychological geometry is a geometry of dichotomies (George Kelly, 197

The difference between the internal and the external spaces is tl
one is objective, meaning stable, the other subjective, meaning tha
is subject to changes and flights of fancies. As Paul Virilio points out,
maybe it was Aristotle, the first has "substance", the other is made
"accidents", things that happen. However, it is key to understand tl
according to the untold principles of alphabetic literacy, the outsi
world be fixed and the inside one totally contained in a mobile bo
That intuition may be what inspired Shakespeare – who, besic
being one of the world's greatest dramatists was also one of its ea
est and best cognitive scientists – to say that the whole world was
a stage, and that all men and women were nothing but actors. T
does not necessarily mean that all men and women are nothing bu
bunch of hypocrites, playacting their roles instead of living real liv
but it certainly means that they are first and foremost actors: in ot
words, people have the power of action, while the world, or "natu
as it were, is the décor, the ground, foreground and background,
theatre where their lives are played and where architecture is built.

Theatre, perspective, theory – and architectural facades – all consp
to create a clear distinction between the objectivity of what one s
and the subjectivity of who does the seeing. The visual bias is pre
cated on a point-of-view. This point of view is unique and establis
the position, both physical and psychological, and also ontologica
the self. The question is to be or not to be. Everything else, as Har
found out, is secondary.

It is in relation to this shape of what must be called the "private mi
and distinguished from either no mind at all, or a kind of collec
mind, that a radically new psychological development is occurr
the formation of the connected mind.

9. Occupy-ability

We have technologically extended our senses to observe objects too small or distant to see directly. The list of such devices is large – ranging from radio and television to digital technologies and computer networks. We are increasingly dependent on such technologies to sustain our social and cultural reality. They are part of being human in our time (Peter Anders, 2000).

Today our very exclusive internal space is being challenged and perhaps already restructured by electronic media, TV, radio, computers and the Internet. Together, these constitute cyberspace. Technically, radio and TV do not "belong" to cyberspace, but now that they are included in the World Wide Web, they provide context, content and support to the cognitive environment that is properly cyberspace.

> With cyberspace, a whole new space is opened up by the very complexity of life on earth: a new niche for a realm that lies between the two worlds. Cyberspace becomes another venue for consciousness itself (Michael Benedikt, 1991)[2].

There is a new continuity between the private mind and the world, but there is also a new connectivity between the private minds in the world. A connected screen is more than a "window on the world", it is a searchlight and a hand right into it. It is also the portal through which minds interact and leave common traces. The private mind is newly connected to other people via cyberspace and that relationship is spatialized as well as specialized. Cyberspace is visible on screen. Otherwise, it is hidden in wires and waves and pulses. It is like the human nervous system, under the skin of culture. It is quite certainly a "space" because it has an inside and an outside (the wired versus the not wired), and a deep interiority (the depths of connectivity and hypertextuality).

Professor Anna Cicognani, from the faculty of architecture at the University of Sidney proposes, among possible others, five criteria to qualify "spaces": 1, the possibility of interaction, by which she means "possible physical transformations inside space", 2, "livability", or "occupy-ability" (the possibility of dwelling in a space), 3, a community-building capacity (which she rightly emphasizes "can exist beyond their geographical location"), 4, time management and 5, space management opportunities[3]. With the arguable exception of "livability", cyberspace qualifies on all these fronts and more.

10. Virtuality

Even the issue of whether cyberspace can be occupied or not is arguable because, as Borre Ludvigsen points out, we "project our presence" into it. And, on the larger scale, it contains us as a total environment made up of many unseen interconnections that make up our space.

Ludvigsen adds:

> Cyberspace is available to anyone and all of us who are capable of consciously projecting our presence into it. Its form takes its cues from our visions of form in digital space, visual or imaginary. It is the 2-dimensional space of drawings, the 3-dimensional space of synthetic models, the n-dimensional space of sound, time and words. Its media are as diverse as the technology involved, spanning from the pulsating columns of mud that carry telemetry from instruments in oil well drilling bits into the networks of oil companies to the very-high speed broadband optical networks of NREN[4].

The Internet and the Web are both virtual, a fact that people who promote VR, often fail to mention. It is the virtuality, not the spatiality of cyberspace, which makes it akin to a mental space. Cyberspace is fluid and inexhaustible like a mind, but it is neither exclusively material nor truly "mental". And certainly, it is entirely different from physical space. It is a single environment, allowing every imaginable combination, permutation and configuration of networks. The mental space is also virtual. Both kinds of spaces require visualization and design, both play with sensorial representations/ simulations. Both are endowed with memory, both have search, retrieve and display mechanisms. Both practise information-processing and both are endowed with intelligence.

Just as the conditions for the best operation of the mind in physical space have been detachment, distance, concentration and focus, the conditions for the optimal operation of the mind in cyberspace are ubiquity, connection, penetration, focused self-organization and common standards, protocols and codes.

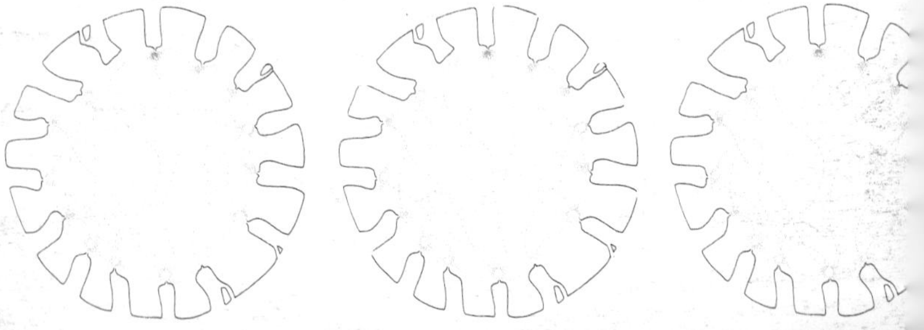

11. Design-based

Cyberarchitecture is henceforth addressed to the positions of the mind as well as to those of the bodies (Roy Ascott, 1995).

What is at stake and what's in it for architecture?

Cyberspace has reached a level of maturation that reveals its consistency, complexity and flexibility. It suggests that it is qualitatively different, and yet partly integrated with the other kinds of "spaces" that people occupy, the physical space and the mental space. It is a third realm between and around and within physical and mental spaces, hence in need of structure and management and thus amenable to architectural considerations. Roy Ascott suggests that:

> To its everyday users, a city is not just a pretty façade. It's a zone of negotiation made up of a multitude of networks and systems. What is needed is designers of such spaces who can provide forms of access which are not only direct and transparent but which enrich the city's everyday business and everyday transactions. The language of access to the processes of communications, production and transformation is more concerned with systems interfaces and network nodes than with traditional architectural discourse.[5]

Anna Cicognani gives four reasons why architects should have a say about the construction of on-line environments:

> a. They are familiar with space organization. b. They are aware of the relationships between space organization and performance. c. They have a good understanding of the design process and its negotiating and executive phases. d. They are used to transforming basic materials into functional elements (e.g. wood/chair, brick/wall)[6].

Peter Anders notes that even before the arrival of computers, architecture and design always alternated between the physical and the mental world with spatial representations as intermediate stages of development:

> Architects and designers – specialists in spatial design – can extend their services once they grasp the power of the symbols they use. Symbols embodied in the computer take on a validity of their own independent of their referential role.

12. Connected Architecture

The urban is a machine that connects and disconnects, articulates and disarticulates, frames and releases (Christian Huebler, 1998).

The need for an architecture of interfaces and nodes will not go away. We shall increasingly live in two worlds, the real and the virtual, and in many realities, both cultural and spiritual (Roy Ascott, 1996).

Indeed, architecture may be just the term that is needed to provide a common ground of exploration and correlation for the three spaces. There may be a need to identify some relationships between the three spaces and especially those that are changing architecture. A better understanding of how it relates to the other two spaces is useful. This is what is meant by "Connected architecture". Connected architecture is not web architecture or "information architecture" as these things already exist and have a large body of available research on them. So what is it? It is the architecture that supports the physical and mental interconnectivity of bodies and minds. Connected architecture is based on the notion that there is such a thing as connected minds and that their connections are supported by technologies that enable them to assemble at specific times to achieve specific goals. Just like "solid" architecture facilitates and guides the coming and going of bodies in space, connected architecture, by the combined use of software and hardware, facilitates the free coming together and parting of minds in collaboration for whatever purpose.

A typical feature of the forms of agency that evolve in networked environments is that they are neither individualistic nor collective, but rather connective. While individualistic and collective diagrams assume a single vector, a single will that guides the trajectory of the action, the connective diagram is mapped onto a machinic assemblage. Whereas the collective is ideally determined by an intentional and empathetic interaction between its components, the connective is an assemblage which is based on any kind of machinic interaction and is therefore more versatile, more open, and based on the heterogeneity of its members. (Knowbotic Research, *10_dencies – Questioning Urbanity*, in *The Art of the Accident*, vol. 2, p. 186).

Connected architecture tackles the management of thresholds and infrastructures between first the physical and the virtual space, but ultimately also the thresholds between mental and virtual spaces even as more and more designers are called upon to interpret its new cognitive possibilities. Bringing the unique skills of their profession, the cyber architects and designers also need to feel comfortable in network management and in psychology. Connected architecture is concerned with the architecture of connections. It is a challenge to discover the structures of networks that are most effective at multiplying mind by mind. It is the architecture of intelligence.

13. Principles

(A city)'s infrastructure, like its architecture, must be both 'intelligent' and publicly intelligible, comprising systems, which react to us, as much as we interact with them. The principle of rapid and effective feedback at all levels should be at the very heart of the city's development. This means high-speed data channels criss-crossing every nook and cranny of its urban complexities (Roy Ascott, 1996).

Principles of interaction between the three spaces

A "principle" is a word that points to an existing or a needed bias in a process. It is a dynamic metaphor, inviting the mind to play the field so to speak. This is why instead of taking ourselves too seriously, and rushing to whittle down our inspirations to a reasonable number of principles, we have decided first to put up all the dynamics potentially implied in connected architecture. The consequence is that what is meant in this book by "principles" is not always the same thing. Sometimes it means biases, such as the "e-principle" or "digitization" which indicate that a strong technologically-driven line-of-force is applied to socio-cultural as well as psychological phenomena. From this kind of dynamics, the word principle is extended to mean trends, such as "convergence", "miniaturization" "decentralization" or "globalization". These trends can, of course, become somewhat prescriptive once they have been recognized, thanks to a kind of socio-cultural recursive and self-amplifying effect. Sometimes a principle simply refers to housekeeping operating practices such as "navigability", "user friendliness", or operating conditions of cyberspace such as "hypertextuality", "interactivity", "virtuality" or "homeopathy" which reminds us that a single tiny bit of news leaked into cyberspace can be instantly available everywhere. In several instances, the words can be taken as rule-of-thumb suggestions, for example, "materiality", implying that one should always look to the material context of anything virtual if one is to succeed in implementing cyber architectural initiatives. The purpose of listing these principles is to challenge the reader to think dynamically because the nature of a principle is to apply a mental organizational force to the object under consideration. The connection between principle, quote, image and text on each page is not always immediate. There is as much fun in verifying and resisting a suggested principle as there is in applying it.

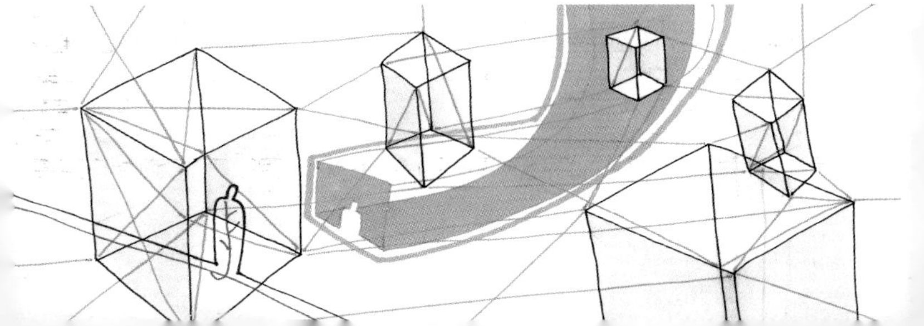

2. Cyberspace and Physical Space

14. Network Sensitivity

The architecture of intelligence is the architecture of networks. It has to deal with several levels of operation and complex interactions between them. One way to understand networks is to think about communities, networks of persons. Today the personal and social networks are supported by a technological extension, a technical surrogate of the Central Nervous System, as McLuhan observed first. Another way to understand networks is to lie flat on your stomach or your back on a large, even and soft surface so that every part of your body that weighs anything is supported. Start paying attention to every tension (this is easier to perform on the stomach than on the back because the dorsal sensations are not affected by the weight of the body). You will soon begin to notice textures and arrays of tensions, pulls and tone that communicate with each other. These feelings emerge from networks of neuromuscular activation that shift and move under the pressure of the attention itself. They are the core of tactility. These networks are susceptible to stress and will sometimes suffer blockages that force them to generate a general strategy of relaxation. So they emerge as a yawn or a stir, two usually spontaneous activities. Of course what you are experiencing is an organic network, seemingly very different from technological ones. Or is it ?

Electronic networks, like the organic ones, are suffused with intelligence. They know how to interact with one another smoothly and efficiently. They are made of complex levels of activities, by people and by machines, by sheer intelligence (software) and concrete interventions, by mixes of conscious and unconscious processes. They bring together distant areas for common activities and they sometimes affect these areas in visible ways. These networks are fairly complex. They bear scrutiny but only reveal group identities with soft edges, and from one to another, very different textures.

15. Emergence

Cyberspace is an emergent phenomenon (Margaret Wertheim, 1999)

The technical networks are grounded in a completely logical-rational infrastructure. On the physicality of cyberspace, Margaret Wertheim comments:

> Ironically, cyberspace is a technological by-product of physics. The silicon chips, the optic fibers, the liquid crystal display screens, the telecommunications satellites, even the electricity that powers the Internet are all by-products of this most mathematical science. Yet if cyberspace could not exist without physics, neither is it bound within the purely physicalist conception of the real. In the parlance of complexity theory, cyberspace is an emergent phenomenon, something that is more than the sum of its parts. This new "global" phenomenon emerges from the interaction of its myriad interconnected components, and is not reducible to the purely physical laws that govern the chips and fibers from which it indubitably springs[7].

Emergence

Cyberspace is a cognitive and intelligent phenomenon that quite literally "emerges" from a grid of so much hardware. I have always found the so-called "mind-brain" duality problem not a problem at all because whenever I am confronted by it, the above analysis is the kind of thing that springs to my mind. I do not see any more mystery in the mind "emerging" from evidently "physical" neurological activities, than Margaret Wertheim, or anyone, for that matter, should to see that the astonishing and still growing complexity of cyberspace is grounded in the irrefutably logical, verifiable and tangible reality of technological networks. The value of this comparison is to alert us to the fact that with cyberspace, a third element, or a third party is added to the interaction between the living organic participation of people's minds and bodies in the space people inhabit. Should we have to invoke some kind of "trinomy" (i.e. material, technological and mental) to account for cyberspace?

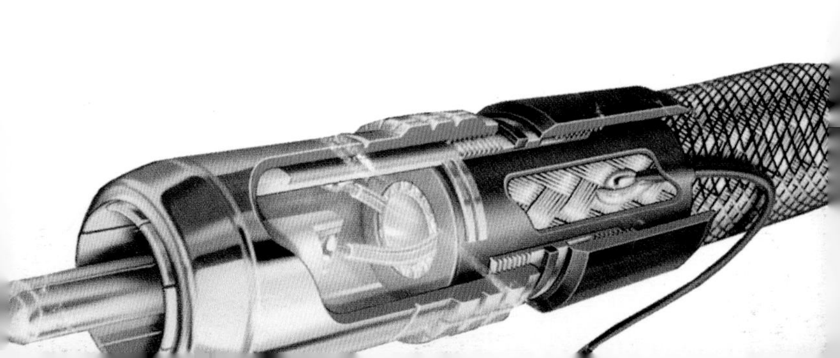

16. A-Principle Versus E-Principle

The e-principle

"Even electricity...". Today, it has become fashionable, not to say tiresome, to put an e in front of e-verything, every word being thus electrified for new energy, new meaning. The e usually stands for "electronic" as in e-mail or e-commerce or e-world. To be truer to the deeper nature of what is happening in the psycho-technological realm, the letter should really stand for "electrical". Electricity has taken the place of the "Prime Mover" in this realm. Shut it off and the whole thing is wiped out like a dream. The Internet is a child of electricity, not of computers. Electricity is imposing its character in all previously held territories of the Industrial age, and even of a much larger age, that of the alphabet. The e-principle is conquering all the domains previously held by the a-principle, that of the alphabet which accompanied and fostered the previous era, the mechanical age. It's smashing everything to bits.

Electrical space

Electricity is the core technology. It has dethroned the domination of the mechanical principle and has reversed many of the explosive and fragmenting tendencies of the alphabet. Electricity is creating a new kind of relationship to space. From the time of the telegraph, electricity has never ceased to contract space and reduce it to a dot, while the alphabet expanded it to infinity. The world of print and the alphabet is centrifugal, with information spatialized and spread all over the map. The printing press distributed books in space and required that information be repeated wherever it was needed, but electricity puts the process of human communications, and much of its content on wires and screens. With electricity the general architecture of information is that it is placed anywhere and available everywhere on demand. It is stored in databases that are instantly retrievable. Electricity's effect on information even as far back as the telegraph was and still is centripetal: wherever you are is the node to which all data arrive.

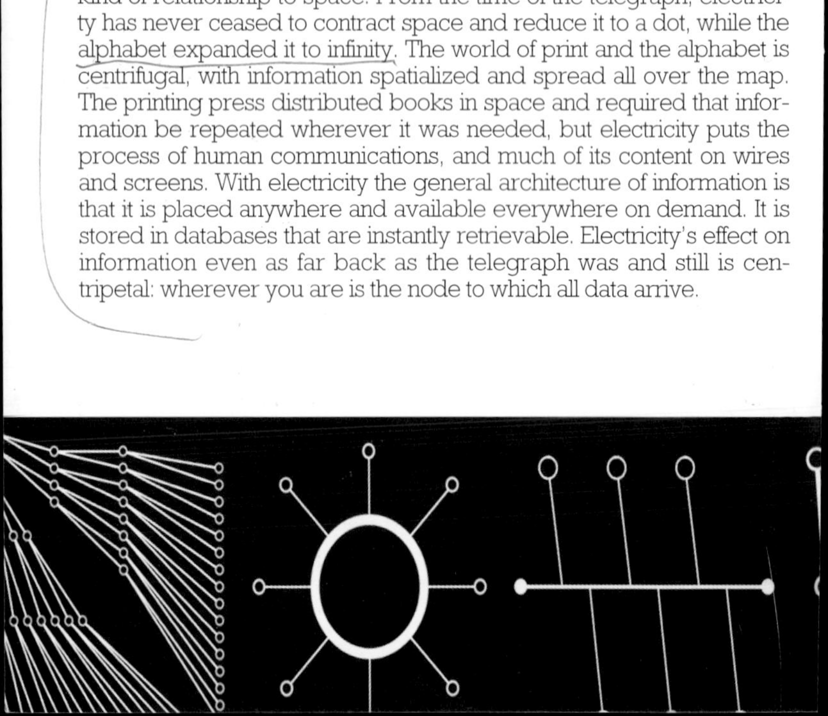

17. Implosion

Electricity has put Humpty Dumpty together again (McLuhan)

If the alphabet split language in many parts and reduced the senses involved in human communication to a string of abstract signs, electricity is bringing all the senses back together again in multimedia, interactive systems and virtual reality. Electricity brings everything together in a flash. Its dynamic is implosive. To Descartes who said: "Give me extension and I will build you a world", the programmer answers: "Give me a chip and I will bring you the world". Electricity is not a visual medium, let's not confuse it with light bulbs, it is tactile. Electricity puts everything in touch just as the alphabet had put everything in perspective. Electricity is immersive. It provides the world in total surround, thus reducing the dominance of frontal relationships, such as were reinforced by reading and writing. Electricity is ubiquitous: it does not traverse space, but the movement of waves and particles (electrons) consists in pushing each other or unfolding everywhere at once.

The tactility of both wired and wireless reflects complementary properties of electricity. The distribution of electronic information reveals the spatial – and sensorial – properties of elecromagnetic fields, which register and transmit instantaneously any disturbance generated at any point in the field. As Wade Rowland explains:

> All electric communication stems from the notion that if electrons can be inducted to flow in a wire or radiate through space, then it ought to be possible to communicate electronically by manipulating the electron flow in such a way as to carry intelligence. By dots and dashes, for example, generated by switching the electron flow on and off. The only trick is to develop suitable electron-generating devices at the transmitting end and appropriate electron-detecting devices at the receiving end. This proved simpler in the case of a wired connection than a wireless link, and wired telegraphy thus preceded wireless telegraphy[8].

The α principle	*The ε principle*
Static	Dynamic
Explosive	Implosive
Visual	Tactile
Frontal	Immersive
Centralized	Distributed
Analog	Digital
Memory-based	Intelligence-based
Specialized	Convergent
Fragmented	Integrated
Abstract (desensorialized)	Multisensory
Spatialized (actualized)	Virtualized
Stepwise, discrete	Continuous

18. Complexity

Electricity is the soul of modern age, information is its spirit (Erik Davis, 1998)[9]

Nodes, modes and codes
It took a hundred and sixty-five years between the invention of the telegraph (1837), the first real application of electricity to transport language and the development of the World Wide Web (1992) which actually processes language in a way comparable if not similar to the way the mind processes it. This began to happen with word-processing, but it is really with hypertext that a truly cognitive relationship between electricity, people and language started.

Language multiplied by the speed of light
The history of how cyberspace got to this point begins with a mythical union, that of language and electricity, the combination of maximum complexity with maximum speed, the speed of light. Just as the printing press was the meeting point of language and mechanization, the telegraph was that of language and electricity. While previous to the electrification of language, the job of books was to accelerate information, their new role, perhaps just as critical for human understanding, is now to slow it down. Indeed, books are now the only place where information does not move.

The existence of cyberspace requires the support of a very complex architecture involving at least three levels of constraints:

1. The hardware architecture of nodes and their connections, namely the electronic grid of the planet, the telegraph, the telephone, computer terminals and all the connecting and processing gear needed to power, transform, transmit and receive data;
2. The media architecture of modes, that is the telegraph, telephone, radio, television, and all the previous media which are now converging on the Internet and which all differ by the kinds of configurations they provide for connecting people and delivering information;
3. The software architecture of codes, the various protocols and standards that allow the formatting and targeted distribution of data.

19. Acceleration

Time for major technologies to reach 50 million users: Radio: 30 years
Tv: 13 years
WWWeb: 4 years

The architecture of nodes

The progression from the epic days of laying the first undersea cables (1857–1866) to today's "dark fibers" and "terabauds" transmission capacities takes two kinds of measurement, speed and volume of activities. The volume increase derives from the number of interconnections while the speed increase concerns the capacity of the lines, the celerity of switchers and the integration of processors. These have followed something like Moore's Law, growing exponentially since the humble 5 bauds of the telegraph. It's as if the planet was wiring itself to start thinking.

Speed and volume

From the telegraph to the telephone, there was a quantum leap in interconnection. But a new quantum leap has been made by the WWW because it not only interconnects everybody but also what everybody is saying. The interconnection of contents, which is the meaning of hypertext, provides for an infinite number of combinations. There is substantial talk of a new development called the "embedded Internet" which would connect all electronic technologies down to the humblest thermostats to the Internet for security, maintenance and monitoring purposes. We can interpret this development as an "electronic straightjacket" or more pertinently as a kind of technological skin as Bells Labs recently described it in a press release on line (Spring 1999):

> We are already building the first layer of a mega-network that will cover the entire planet like a skin. As communication continues to become faster, smaller, cheaper and smarter in the next millennium, this skin, fed by a constant stream of information, will grow larger and more useful. That skin will include millions of electronic measuring devices – thermostats, pressure gauges, pollution detectors, cameras, microphones – all monitoring cities, roadways, and the environment. All of these will transmit data directly into the network, just as our skin transmits a constant stream of sensory data to our brain.

Transmission speeds on line
1837: telegraph: 5 bps (bauds per second)
1877: telephone: 2,000 bps
1892: underwater cables: 2,500 Kbps (kilo bauds per second)
1945: coaxial cable: 9Mbps (mega bauds per second, a million bits of data stream per second)
Transmission speeds via modem
1960: 1st modem: 300bps
1984: Hayes "Smartmodem": 1,200bps (1.2Kbps)
1986: NSFNET: 56Kbps
1988: T1: 1,500,000bps (1.5Mbps)
1991: T3: 45 Mbps
1996: ATM lines (A-synchronous Transfer Mode): 622 Mbps
2000+: Dark fiber (gigabauds, terabauds, petabauds and beyond)

20. Interconnectivity

Networks are simultaneously real, like nature, narrated, like discourse, and collective, like society (Bruno Latour)

Three webs

On top of the power grid, the wiring of the planet's information system was accomplished with three integrated, but technically superposed "webs", the telegraph cables, the telephone switchboards and the WWW.

> To review:
> *Telegraph* = city-to-city
> *Telephone* = building-to-building
> *Wireless* = body-to-body
> *Internet* = everybody-to-everybody
> *World Wide Web* = content-to-content
> *Embedded Internet* = every tool connected to the Internet behaving as a central processing unit.

At this level of interactivity, something emerges from the overall pattern, and we begin to talk about "cyberspace". It is interesting that an artist, William Gibson, one of the most prescient of science-fiction writers, created the term, almost a decade before the Web was realized. On the other hand, the concept had already emerged, so to speak, in the mind of another creator, Ted Nelson, who invented the term "hypertext". While it is clear that all media are now converging on-line, a new set of constraints is fast developing "on air" so to speak, namely the architectures of satellite and cellular communications. If you bring on-line and wireless distribution systems together, you fill all available space with the presence of intelligence, a bit like the Gods of Antiquity...

The architecture of modes

The convergence of all media on line that reflects the implosive dynamics of the ε-principle spells the end of the mass experience, but not necessarily the end of the individual media themselves. Different media propose different configurations of use and of social groupings. From the isolated stance of the silent reader, repeated by the stand-alone computer in electronic terms, to the convergent hypermedia which bring the benefits of radio, TV, print and data on the same platform, each medium has created its own dynamic from the moment it was introduced. Such dynamics fall into three categories:

One-way (radio, TV)
Two-way (telecommunications, telephone)
My-way (Internet, Web)

21. Wirelessness

The Copernican Revolution transformed the earth quite literally into a mobile home (Karsten Harries, 1998).[10]

One-way media produce, store and deliver content that has a quick obsolescence and a low re-use rate. They are modeled on the printing press and on the architecture of the Industrial Revolution. They produce for the masses as much as they can. Now, as they are being threatened to be superseded by the Internet, they become the easy targets of those who advocate taking control of the screen. They perform, however, an important and often underestimated social function, which is to bring everybody together for a while. "Passive" consumers of TV become active participants in a collective consciousness that is predicated precisely on the fact that everybody is receiving the same information at the same time. They provide occasions for community in cyberspace. Radio will retain its strong identity because it doesn't require the user to stay still, just like the mobile phone. But, of course, the difference between a Walkman radio and a mobile phone is that if I get radio via earphones, the world occupies me, but if I call anywhere I want in the world, I occupy the world.

Cyberspace is public space
The Internet and the Web are MY-WAY media, and it doesn't matter how much of cyberspace is occupied by business or government, whatever forms these take in the future, or how much smut there really is on-line or how many Intranets are preventing my access to whosoever. What matters is that as long as there is that public space out there, that public cyberspace, something that we all share and that has infinite expandability, we will always have a room there, a position and a reality that depends only on us.

Wirelessness
Wireless technologies change our relationships to physical space because they dilate and dilute human gatherings instead of bringing them together in one point. The cellular phone is the most intimate of all our communication technologies, although some people might say also the noisiest and the most intrusive.

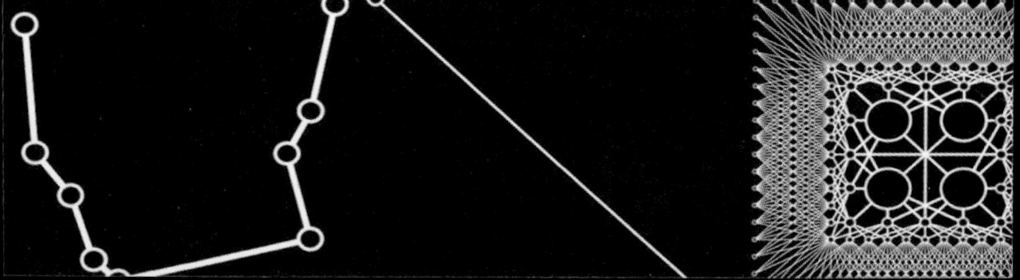

22. Proprioception

The mobile phone heralds the return of our extended CNS into our body

Because it can be carried all the time, the cellular phone is the communication device closest to the body. It gives freedom of movements, allowing one to carry one's files, concerns, office, connections, d-bases on one's body. It is a direct extension of touch, vision and hearing, a probing and roaming device for worldwide navigation. The cellular phone is quite literally a new sensory organ. Technology has this way of becoming an indispensable part of the flesh. If McLuhan was right about electricity as the worldwide extension of the CNS, then the cellular phone spells the return of the electronic grid surrounding the planet right into the body. The cellular phone is the privileged connection of my being with the world at large.

The cellular phone is also very comprehensive; it is the technology that underlines and supports best our new mental scale that is global. When it is truly globalized, it will be the instrument that will change the scale of people's individual notions of themselves. Cellular technology does what radio couldn't, that is to fill the space of the airwaves with MY presence, at least my potential presence. Suddenly the space of communications is really mine, just like the physical space. I can carve my spot in it. At the same time, the cellular phone supports the image of space as a permeable environment, extending it to the limits of reachability of the calls. It supports the image of the individual body in space as having a point of origin, it supports a kind of "point-of-being" that complements the use and properties of a "point-of-view".
It could be that we retrieve at the techno-cultural level the most ancient categories of human societies, the e-nomads who are carrying the world in their pocket, and the e-sedentaries who are surfing the world from their home or their office without moving their feet. The difference is that space invades e-sedentaries, while e-nomads invade space. It's a matter of taste.

23. Codicity

The architecture of codes

There are two levels in the software architecture of codes that provide for two varieties of infrastructures: one could be called the "Internet plumbing" code which regulates its basic operation and is guided by the principle of efficiency; the other is the growing quantity of possible applications which can be coded to become effective on line.

By the middle 90s, most of the basic technical infrastructure, the software architecture to get the Internet up and running, had been put in place. What remains to examine is not the technical software which was and remains geared to maximum network efficiency and maximum access at all levels, technological, financial and cognitive, but what one might call the "behavioral" architecturing of the Internet, which, according to Lawrence Lessig is the proper realm of the code.

> The rules governing any computer-constructed micro world are precisely and rigorously defined in the text of the program that constructs it on your screen (William Mitchell, 1995).

In Code, his brilliant study of the "laws of cyberspace", Lessig uses the term architecture quite liberally, and claims "code is law". He suggests that it is precisely the architecture of the code that constrains the shape and usages of cyberspace:

> The software and hardware that make cyberspace what it is constitute a set of constraints on how you can behave. The substance of these constraints may vary, but they are experienced as conditions on your access to cyberspace. [...]. The code or software or architecture or protocols set these features; they are features selected by code writers; they constrain some behavior by making other behavior possible, or impossible. The code embeds certain values or makes certain values impossible. In this sense, it too is regulation, just as architectures of real-space codes are regulations[11].

Such regulatory measures come into play when a medium such as radio, television or the Internet moves from the periphery of the economy to its center.

24. IDENTITY

Code is law (Lawrence Lessig, *1999*)

While in its early years, much of what happened to develop the Net amounted to a kind of "focused self-organizing principle", by which I mean an unplanned but effective task-oriented combination of existing resources, innovations and trial-and-error, too much is at stake today to leave the Internet to chance. At least, that is the point-of-view supported by Lessig. The main areas that require a governing attention, in his opinion, are intellectual property (IP), privacy, free speech and sovereignty. Not all are equally amenable or require the same level of regulation, but all need attention for fear of losing the benefits of the Internet.

Thus the Internet is both grounded in real space and also virtual. But the virtual is just as "real" and constraining as the real. We have to get used to this concept to fully understand why there is as much need for architectural considerations when it comes to bits and bytes as when we are talking bricks and mortar. Code alone is responsible for such things as firewalls and encryption to protect data from unwanted intrusion. Likewise, code creates intranets, virtual networks that are impenetrable by visitors external to the business. By structuring the circulation, storage and access of data, code also regulates behavior. Just as urban planning and residential architecture de facto regulate the movements and affect the behavior of the people who live there.

Lessig examines attentively the code that regulates access and certifies identity in what he calls "architectures of identification", namely the ID, the password, the most common identifiers and then, the "cookie", a file sitting in your computer, containing relevant data about you to keep your supplier informed about your specific needs. That way, whenever you order another book from *Amazon.com*, the distributor knows everything needed to accelerate delivery.

25. Privacy

The more they know about you, the less you exist (Marshall McLuhan)

Lessig does not advocate banning the use of cookies. On the contrary, he rightly points out that they are extremely valuable in the myriad cases where the information is not sensitive, but just useful. The question here is: who else might want to know as much about you and for what purposes? Other suppliers, or the government, or the mafia, can also gain access to your cookies. This problem is not new. The moment you pay anything via credit card, something about you is known and presumably available to other interests. Just imagine the seamless combination of barcode accounting, credit card payment and automated cross-referencing that allows credit operators to get your profile and know more about you than, in that respect at least, you know yourself. McLuhan foresaw this private information circulation as one of the major threats not only to privacy, but also to identity itself. The philosophical underpinning of this statement is that the e-principle, quite contrary to the a-principle, is not at all in favor of private identity. Forget the panopticon, we may be subjected to a kind of permanent, automated e-nquisition that ultimately will turn us inside out, our souls bared for electronic inspection by a code. The average citizen in a democracy certainly needs protection against that.

Intellectual property is a concomitant issue arising only when a full consciousness of identity is available. One day, after generations of anonymous – and spectacularly talented – artists had built the European cathedrals entirely without personal recognition, another church commissioned sculptor, named Michelangelo decides to sign his work: "Hoc fecit Michelangelo" is written on the marble of his justly celebrated Moses. This is an instance of private identity surfacing, as it should during the Renaissance, the time of the "second birth" of the individual in Western Europe.

26. Intellectual Property

Information wants to be free (John Perry Barlow, 1995)

Intellectual property has become big business in the age of information because it is pure information. People, who appropriate the common English language, not to develop their private selves but to serve as brands and virtual real estate, register even domain names. The point is precisely that IP is not necessarily related to a private subject (although in many cases it is and will remain so), but to a corporate one or to a digital persona.

What Lessig recommends to get both the benefit of security and improved communication with information and service suppliers is what he calls the "digital certificate", "a kind of passport on the Internet":

> Digital certificates would reside on your computer (under at least some designs); a server would automatically (and invisibly) check the certificate as you entered the site. If you held the right certificate, you would be let in, and as you were let in, the server would then "know" the certified facts about you[12].

There are many issues related to copyright and IP that affect the law more than the architecture of codes, but recent developments such as Napster.com, Freenet.com and Gnutella do point to architectural features of the Internet that are changing the rules. The point is that the trend towards freeloading IP is here to stay; notwithstanding court injunctions which are only stopgap measures allowing the industry to rethink copyright practices.

> For citizens of cyberspace, computer code... is the medium in which intentions are enacted and designs realized, and it is becoming a crucial focus of political contest. Who shall write the software that increasingly structures our daily lives? What shall the software allow and prescribe? (William Mitchell, *City of Bits*, p. 112).

The World Internet Society, the ICANN group, the Electronic Frontier Foundation, and other reasonably democratic institutions ensure that the standards, code and protocols of this architecture of intelligence remain open and common.

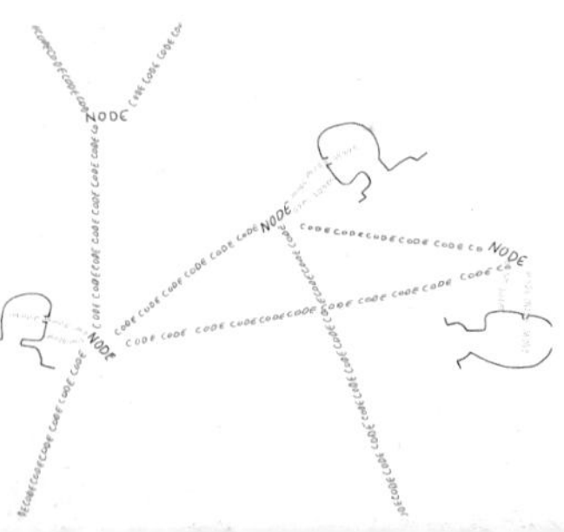

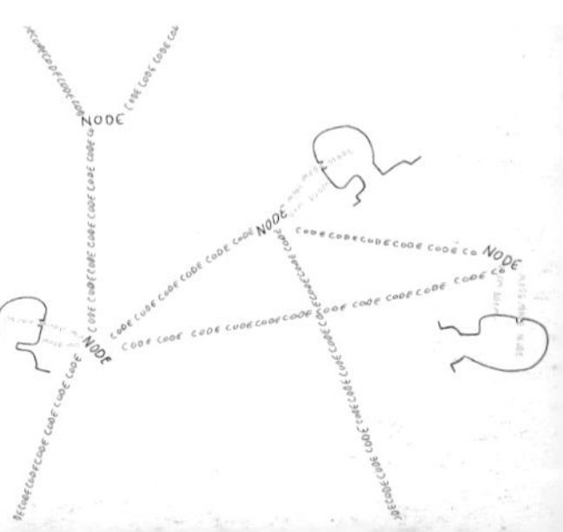

3. Cyberspace and Mental Space

27. Cyberceptivity

We are all interface. We are computer-mediated and computer enhanced (Roy Ascott)

Roy Ascott coined the term "cyberception". The fate of that word in standard English is not decided but it provides a perfect entry into the critically important matter of interfaces and its relevance to renewed thinking in architecture and design. As Ascott puts it:

> The emergent faculty of cyberception, our artificially enhanced interactions of perception and cognition, involves the transpersonal technology of global networks and cyber media. We are learning to see afresh the processes of emergence in nature, the planetary media-flow, while at the same time re-thinking possibilities for the architecture of new worlds. Cyberception not only implies a new body and a new consciousness but a redefinition of how we might live together in the interspace between the virtual and the real.[13]

Five key features of cyberspace and cyberception are brought together in this highly condensed definition: it is global, cognitive, computer-assisted, interspatial and invites architectural considerations. The notion underlying cyberception is that it is potentially global. Notwithstanding the well-known fact that to this day only a fraction of humanity has access to cyberspace in its narrow sense (i.e. the Internet), and the fact that most users may neither require nor take advantage of the opportunity of "going global", the globality of cyberception is a defining and relevant attribute of our new modality of perception. Cyberception could be understood as the third modality of human perception, after the collective discourse of the oral community and the private mind of the literate person. Cyberception is not restricted to the Internet or the web, but ought to include all the means of telesensory inputs and outputs including the old fashioned ones such as the telephone, radio and television, which receive a new meaning in this new context.

28. Technopsychology

> *By creating an interface between the self, the other, and the world beyond, media technologies become part of the self, the other, and the world beyond* (Erik Davis, 1998).

This understanding should not be discouraged by the fact that, as Ascott underlines, cyberception is also computer-assisted. Even in the heart of the jungle, perception is never independent from cultural constraints or from rudimentary technology.

Ascott recognizes better than most the biologically integrated nature of computer-assisted perception. Why would we refuse to acknowledge the fact that our personal organic senses are being extended when we access visually the infinitely small with electron microscopes or the infinitely large with satellite imagery both requiring computer imaging enhancement techniques? If we can accept that eyeglasses are legitimately enhancing and refining our access to the unquestionable evidence of what we see, then we are invited to consider computer-enhanced sensory modalities as further extensions of our private access to heretofore-inaccessible realms. The fact that we can henceforth work on systems and interfaces that allow pertinent access and understanding of both local and global situations, whatever the context or the use we may wish to put such perceptions to, is crucial for the full maturation of both technology and psychology. The issue becomes inevitable once our access is no longer limited to poking the planet with visual and auditory extensions such as television and radio, but henceforth also enabled for action and reaction, with tools such as the telephone and the Internet. Cyberception includes all the interfaces we need to connect with cyberspace. Every tool, and every possibility afforded by the computer is a cognitive extension that highlights the independence and furthers the creative capability of the user. This approach puts the emphasis on interfaces insofar as it is necessary for ordinary people to have easy and fruitful access to cyberspace.

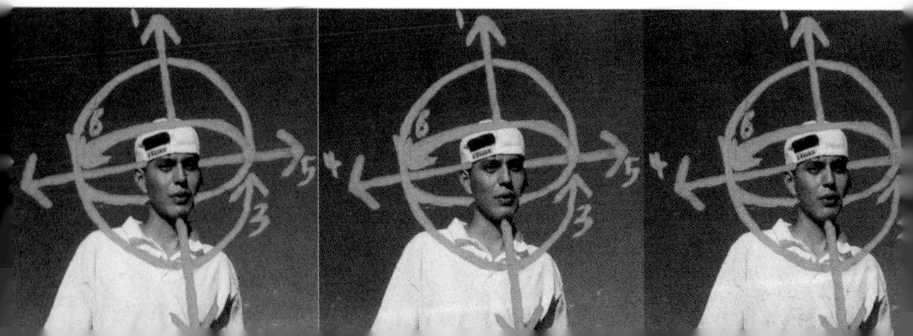

29. Tooling

We are entering an era of electronically extended bodies living at intersection points of the physical and virtual worlds… (William Mitchell, 1995).

The tools of cyberception

A single team of researchers invented practically all the principal tools of cyberception during a short period of time. In June 67, Doug Engelbart, a researcher at Stanford Research Institute (SRI) registered a patent for the mouse, "an x-y position indicator for a visualization system". In a legendary presentation, Englebart and his team demonstrated beside the mouse, a word processor, an interface which would become windows, hypertextual links, a graphical user interface and, as if it were an afterthought, videoconferencing. Engelbart recounts the moment of the original inspiration in the early Sixties:

> When I saw the connection between a television-like screen, an information processor, and a medium for representing symbols to a person it all tumbled together in about half an hour. I went home and sketched a system in which computers would draw symbols on the screen and I could steer through different information spaces with knobs and levers and look at words and data and graphics in different ways.[14]

Screenology

Chief among the tools of cyberception is the screen. Since early in the year 2000, people in North America have begun to spend more time, on average, in front of a computer screen than a television screen. More than half of that computer time happens to be on line. In less than a decade, it is believed that, with the exception of sleeping time, about one fifth of people all over the world will be spending about half as many hours in front of a screen as they will in physical space. A sizeable portion of that time will be devoted to activities structured by and within cyberspace. Just as in the era when TV reigned supreme, much of people's mental activities were occupied by television fare, much of people's occupational and professional activities will happen on line.

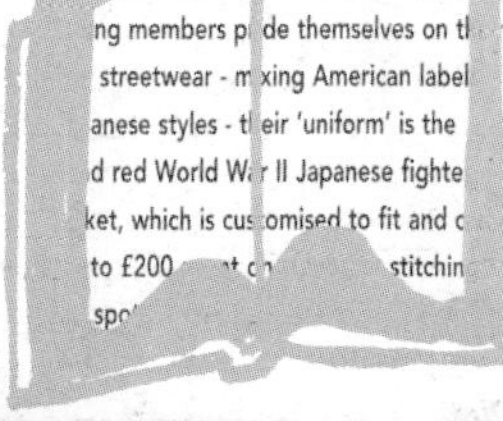

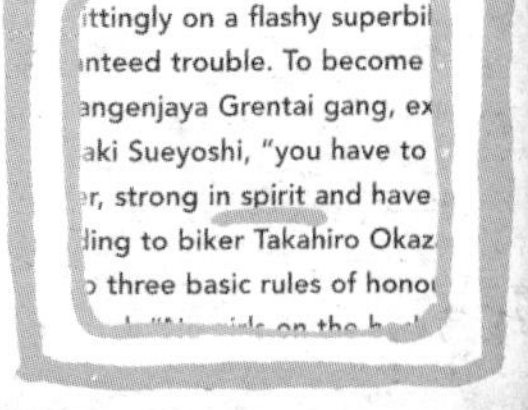

30. Inverted Retina

The screen is the point of coincidence where the physical space of the hardware, the mental space of the user's mind and cyberspace coincide. The screen is also the terminal display area where all networking reaches its end. Just as paper, pens and books were accelerators for information processing in private minds, screens are connectors and accelerators for connected minds.

In the architecture of nodes, the screen is "where the action is". Its content is both cognitive and the object of cognition. Marcos Novak makes a useful distinction between screens of *projection* (as in "display"), of *protection* (as in "screening somebody from the press"), and of selection (filters, biases). While code handles protection and *selection* in cyberspace, the screens of projection unite the three basic spatial environments, they impart a new bias in architecture. To begin with, they change its definition.

When it gives access to the Web, the screen (in whatever shape it comes) is a window on the cognitive contents of the world. Its role could be likened to that of the human retina because it too allows the building of images that reflect both the recording of visual evidence and the processing of strategies of perception and interpretation.

Just as images are not simply reflected in our minds but always built in our brains, the images on the screen are the result of a continuous stream of processing. The human retina is made of brain cells, which are located within the eye at the periphery of the body. Thus the rods and cones that receive and process vision are the most externalized of brain cells. Likewise, the photons or pixels that display the contents of screens are the most externalized elements of the hugely complex and ever-changing organization of cyberspace. The parallel between screens and retinas is made more pertinent by the new field of "vitrionics" or "retinal scanning displays", that is video display systems that project images into the human retina either from eyeglasses or even via contact lenses.

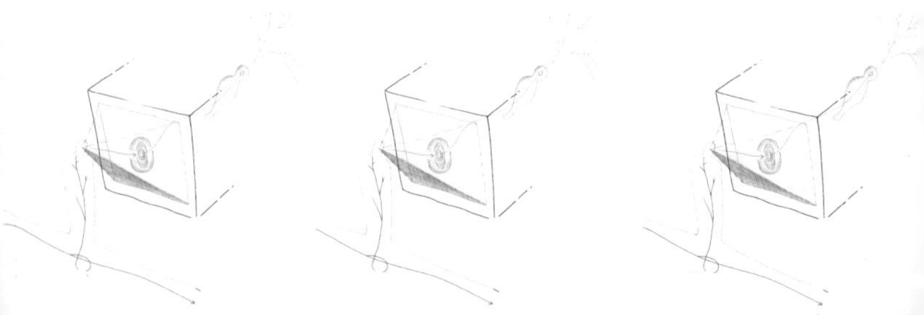

31. Eye Versus Screen Dominance

Without spatialisations, topological structure data are almost impossible for humans to interpret (Martin Dodge and Rob Kitchin, 2001).

In Microvision's words: "Horizontal and vertical scanners 'paint' an image on the eye by rapidly moving the light source across and down the retina, in a raster pattern" (*http://www.mvis.com/1-hiwork.htm*). Sitting in front of our screens, we establish a kind of retinal communication from screen to eye. Millions of screens around the globe provide quasi "synaptic" connections with millions of minds exchanging information. The interval between the screen and the eye is the area of flexibility and interpretation. One obvious difference between passive and interactive relationships with our screens is that interactive systems make full use of this interval for innovation and self-affirmation. By pushing the same content in the mind of huge groups of people at once and at the same time, TV does not allow much flexibility of interpretation. Interactive systems do because they establish a dialogue between each individual user and the system. Innovation arises from the details of our dialogues with programs and people.
Word-processing is a simple example of detailed interaction with the externalized contents of our minds on the screen. Each change entails a creative process. The same goes for desktop editing or graphic design on screen. Of course, there is a kind of dialogue going on between the pen and paper and the writer, but it isn't quite so flexible, nor does it give access to other resources such as databases or even humbler tools such as word count, spell check, formatting and the like. What you write on the screen is already a kind of "publication" by the fact that it is there, fully formatted, presentable as a printed page and ready to post on line if you care to do so. And, as soon as it is on line, it is not only "published", but also available everywhere at once.
It may be the connective quality of screen-based information exchange that reveals the deeper purpose of screen technology in general. Indeed, information processing before the relatively recent development of interactive systems was limited to the space of the mind. That space is entirely private. Screens, apart from face-to-face meetings, of course, are the only devices that allow this meeting of minds literally, to say nothing of the archiving support systems, which enable people to store and retrieve the patterns of their collaboration.

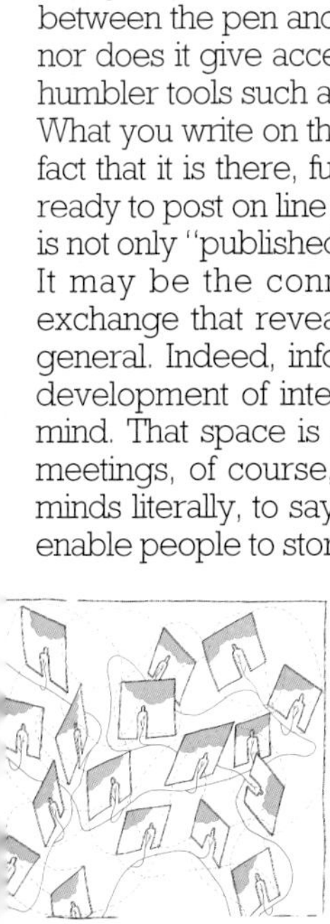
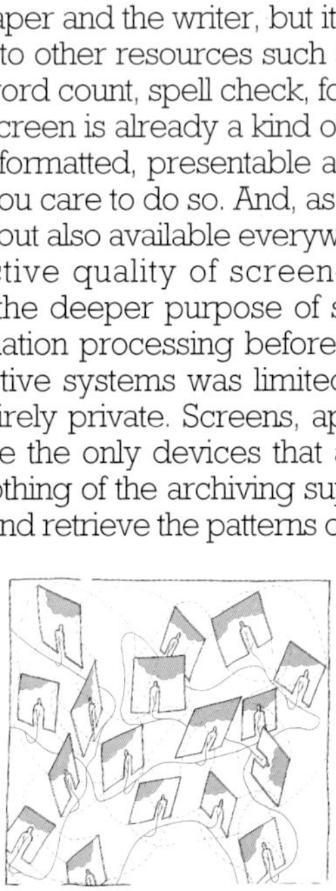
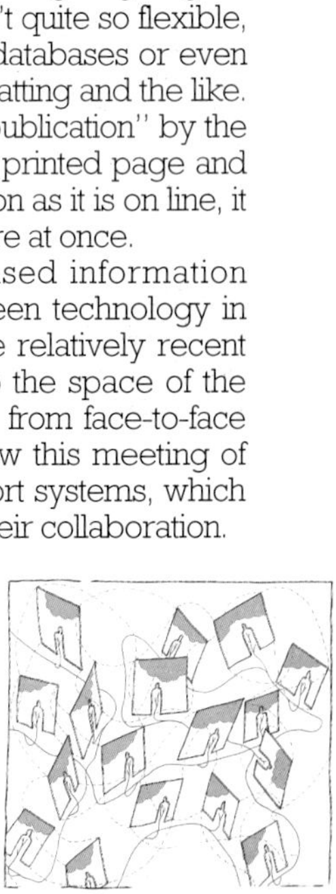

32. Tactility

The mighty mouse: the hand in the mind

The digital era is focused on the digit, from digitus, the word for finger in Latin. This may be an accident, but certainly one that carries a deeper significance in that as we project mind and hand into screens, we are shifting from a visual dominance to a tactile one.

After the screen, the second key technology for cyberspace interfaces is the mouse. We might be tempted to put the keyboard before the mouse since the keyboard is the more articulate of the two. However, as Doug Engelbart observed, for the interaction to be truly effective, the tool must allow the user to actually penetrate the world of information, not merely to send it commands.

Graphical User Interfaces

When GUIs and icons were introduced, along with the mouse, the screen became a world to be explored freely with objects that responded to a click and obeyed. The free roaming mouse liberated the rigid movements of the arrow keys, and the pointer felt like a direct extension of the eye, or the mind. The mouse and pointer connection on the screen is like a hand in the external mind digging, grabbing, pushing, replacing, removing, and allowing a concrete operation followed closely by the eyes and the mind of the user. It is like touching ideas.

Icons and buttons are actors, they are like thoughts, they perform commands instantly. Pointer, mouse, hand and thought work together to effect a change on the screen, the externalized object of my attention. The cybernetic loop between the screen and the mind brings the hand into play, as if the hand were in the mind. The pointer itself is a visual representation of the focusing device I must have in my mind although I can only see its effects, not its cause. Computer technology seems to aim at making visible processes that are effected instantly without apparent interfacing in one's own mind. This novel cognitive operation involves a seamless link between my mind, my body, the computer and, if I am on line, the network.

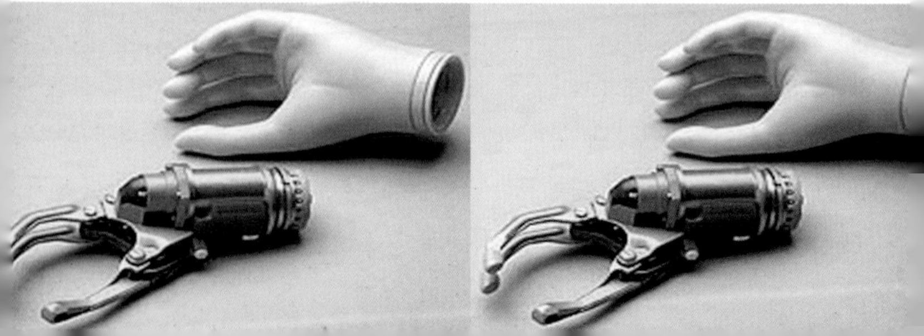

33. Mind-Screen Interaction

When I am surfing the Web, the tactile dimension of clicking and penetrating layers and layers of information feels like the multisensorial process of thinking. I caress images on the screen as I caress thoughts in my mind, shifting from one to the other, focusing here, deleting there. The links work like associations and are in fact associations both in a purely technical way, and also as the result of a "web-assisted" association device, in a psychotechnical way, since mental associations that are supported by what appears on the screen inspire the links that I choose to follow.

This interpenetration of screen and mind is what is new in cyber architecture and its impact on our methods and strategies of personal information processing may be as dramatic as the effect of writing. Just as writing externalized language and thus made it available for meaning production and management, externalizing not only the content but also the process of our thinking both in terms of images and of words makes it available for examination, corrections and reformulation.

Hypertextuality

It seems as if all the stunning innovations presented by Doug Engelbart and his team were different facets of a single powerful intuition: computers were extensions of the mind and the tools to access them should take their inspiration from the way we access the contents of our own thinking. This was basically the intuition of Vannevar Bush in his famous essay of 1945, *As we may think*. The title says it all. Bush was an engineer who had set himself the task of sorting and retrieving useful information from ever increasing quantities of data. The breakthrough came from a shift of perspective on information retrieval. The principle of his project Memex was not to access data hierarchically in alphabetical or numerical order, but through associations between the texts themselves.

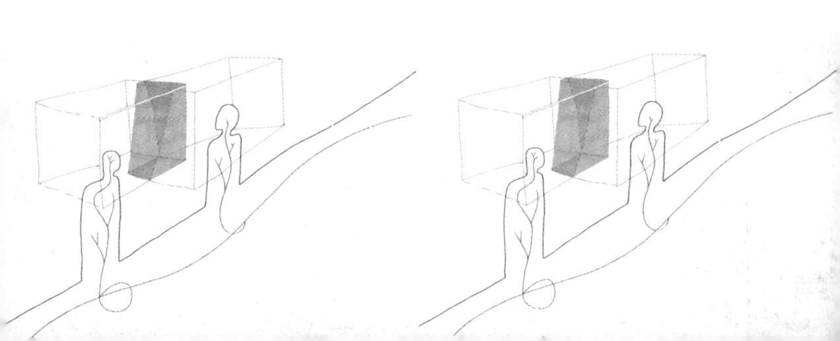

34. WINDOWING

> *The computerization of culture leads to the spatialization of all information, narrative, and, even, time* (Lev Manovich, 1966).

As Landow would point out later[15], the basic intuitions of Bush were to recognize reading as an active rather than passive activity and also that the text should be rethought as a virtual rather than a material or physical entity. However, the fundamental principle of Memex, which would later be formalized in HTML (Hyper Textual Markup Language), was the internal addressing system based on associations between texts. Ted Nelson was on the same track when, during the early Sixties, he invented the term, the principles and most of the architecture of the World Wide Web in the Xanadu project. But Nelson himself never completed the project. Soon after he developed his ideas, Ivan Sutherland demonstrated the first usable window in Sketchpad (1962).

Only Engelbart's refinement of the principles of Windows and the logic of layering allowed the full development of hypertextuality. Combined with the access by mouse-and-pointer, the spatial distribution of information avoids the unilinear dimension of reading and allows in-depth navigation of documents and texts. Spatializing information is something which especially suits those among us who have a good pictorial memory of words on a page. In the window, the pointer is our "point-of-being", our reference point as we immerse ourselves deeper and deeper in the layers of hypertextual data. A window, beside being a kind of opening in dataspace, is always in itself a kind of browser, a system that allows movement inside a virtual environment, a world that is made entirely of virtual objects.

By comparison with the way we can substitute one thought or one image by another in our head, windows may appear clumsy, pedestrian even, but they are very effective precisely because they make apparent and retrievable in a reliable way on our screens a kind of information that is generally hidden, half-formed and constantly changing in our minds.

35. Hypertextuality

[Hypertext] *is a bold and radical idea: a new kind of reading and writing, similar to the old one, but faster, complete with quotes, excerpts and footnotes. It will evolve in time into a vast navigable network, a new literature* (Ted Nelson, 1962).

The fact that hypertext and Windows were invented at the same time marks the evolution of the computer from a merely calculating machine to a mind machine. The GUI was a system to enable dialogue between man and machine based no longer on words, but on icons, that is graphic metaphors. Likewise, hypertext allowed users to bypass the linear and hierarchical constraints of organizing information to display it as a network, open to direct access and susceptible to interconnections via associations. This evolution was followed by the development of the World Wide Web, which in itself, was simply an extension of the principle of hypertextuality to different interconnected databases instead of its original limitation to a single local source. It was henceforth already implicit in the intuitions of Bush, Nelson and Engelbart. In line with his predecessors, Tim Berners-Lee explains:

> The dream behind the Web is of a common information space in which we communicate by sharing information. Its universality is essential: the fact that a hypertext link can point to anything, be it personal, local or global, be it draft or highly polished. I was trying to coordinate many people in many different labs, all working together on distributed processing projects. CERN (Centre Européen des Recherches Nucléaires) is a fairly anarchic environment – a bunch of physicists, all working for different institutes. And I found that a lot of the management was communication, just sharing knowledge, keeping up-to-date your common view of what's going on. So the idea was that it should be interactive, and that it had to be hypertext, because when you're working in the real world, you find connections all over the place.[16]

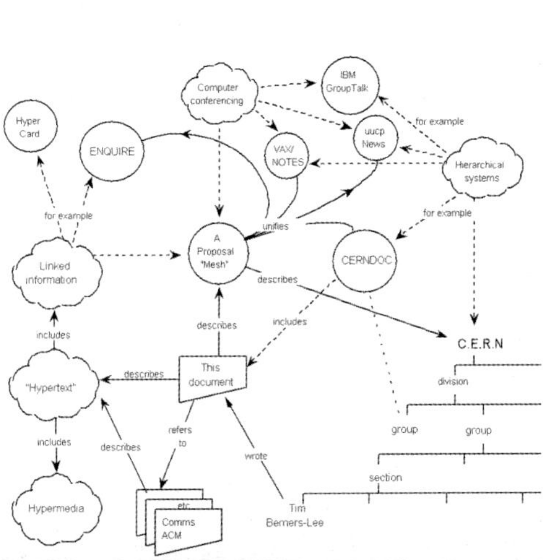

36. Navigability

> *Cyberception means getting a sense of a whole, acquiring a bird's eye view of events, the astronaut's view of the earth, the cybernaut's view of systems* (Roy Ascott).

The concept of navigation extends the metaphor of cyberspace, the "space of the pilot" (actually, the Greek word "kuber" really means "rudder", but, by extension it also refers to piloting), to the strategies to manage it. After all it is still a fluid environment where there is a starting point and there are many possible destinies, not all equally desirable. Apart from the features that come with the browser, including windows, frames, scrolling, bookmarking, backpaging, menus and toolbars, which are issues of steering rather than truly navigating, there are two basic categories of navigational tools, search engines and cybermaps.

Cyber geography

Geography may be one of our most intuitive and decipherable accesses to space on a large scale. We learn to integrate space in the first years of school by looking at maps and copying them. Thus the geographical metaphor is one that makes cyberspace readable, even if it also enforces a bias of spatiality, which, of course, is not there to support the representations. It is easy to forget that in cyber geography, the only space that matters is what room is left on your screen or in your hard disk. As long as we keep that in mind, we can safely visit *http://www.cybergeography.org/atlas/*, the URL for Martin Dodge's magnificent collection of cyberspatial and terrestrial representations. It will reveal an astounding variety of maps for different purposes to help people navigate on and even off line. The first maps on the Web were designed to access sites connected with real space. Virtual Tourist.com, which is not included in Dodge's collection was my introduction to navigation and I still feel a kind of fondness for this simple but effective map of the world showing clickable cities and countries to retrieve sites corresponding to the place.

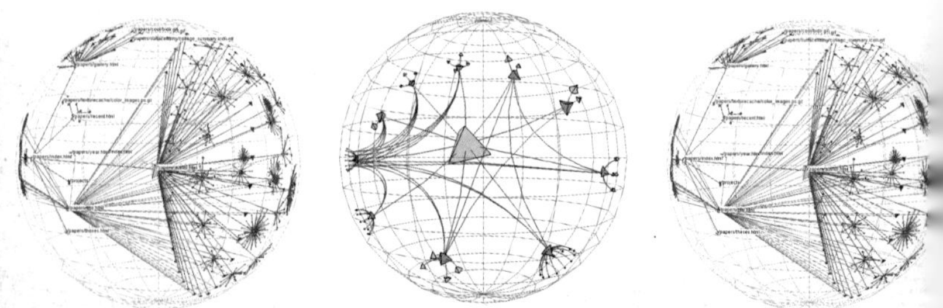

37. CYBERMAPPING

Some geographically grounded maps are directly connected with sensors or webcams which either show online or give a streaming update of flow and traffic density in specific areas, such as the San Diego area free-way system. Cyber geography is also amenable to representing complex statistical information as it pertains to specific locations. The artist Ingo Gunther has thus created a series of globes showing unexpected and often moving figurations of data pertaining to specific regions of the Earth, matters such as levels of literacy, strife, movements of refugees, etc. However, cyber geography is different from terrestrial geography in that it addresses Internet and Web activities on the globe, in regional and local areas. There are many different kinds of maps of Web traffic and internet topologies. There are maps of trace routes for the data transfer and even maps of surfing patterns. Other maps use data for representing different kinds of concentrations of information. Two examples are CATIA's "NewsMaps" which show the concentration of reports on current news as different levels of relief in an island-like territory and Martin Wattenberg's elegant Mondrian-like "Map of the Market" which gives a regular update of the rise and fall of stocks according to selectable categories of investment opportunities. Others address volume in terms of connectivity, that is the number and the history of links to a specific topic or group of issues. There is something moving in seeing information nodes structured in a sphere, such in Tamara Munzner's beautiful data-base navigation tool.

Perhaps among the most frequently accessed kind of territorial representation is the site map, that is, a representation of the architecture of information contained in a specific site, or the rational presentation of linkages. This device allows the user to find both the location and the relationships between various items contained by a site.

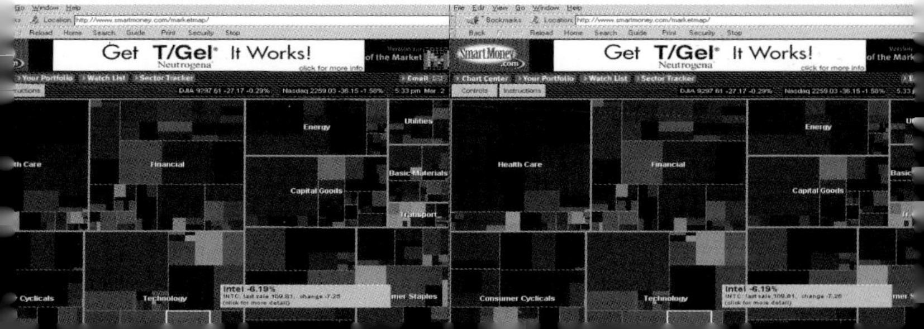

38. Rhizome Formation

A session in cyberspace is a rhizomatic map of itself (Staples, 1995).
Rather than being external to a representation of data, we are navigating links within data (Martin Dodge and Rob Kitchin, 2001).

Among the most striking examples of this category are the Brain, a dynamic text-based relational navigation tool, and *Starrynight, Rhizome.com.* This superb and very user-friendly tool not only helps one to find what there is in this magazine's considerable database, but also to get an instant idea of how different themes connect simply by clicking on any one of the stars that fill the dark blue sky. These and other kinds of database illustrations allow the user to obtain an overview of document concentrations or relationships among different areas of interest. Perhaps the nicest thing about cyber geography is that whatever the term is applied to, there is always implicit in it, the compatibility of virtual, and real and mental spaces.

Search engines
Search engines are the indispensable cognitive tools of cyberspace. They correspond to our own querying abilities, both mentally and socially. Since the invention of Yahoo! in 1994, an invention that is almost as critical for the development of the Web as that of MOSAIC, search engines have developed at ever higher levels of sophistication. There are different categories and their differences are based on the way they carve or "mine" the available information. The basic types of searching tools are directories and "search engines". In directories, such as Yahoo!, the links are not automated but the data is entered in hierarchically sorted categories by people. Crawlers are truly "search engines" in that they automatically scan a site for a keyword or a group of keywords and hop or crawl from site to site via links. Some so-called hybrid or meta search engines combine automation and data-entry by real people. Meta-engines provide simultaneous access to several complementary search engines performing keyword as well as category searches, and responding to a variety of commands to help define the search.

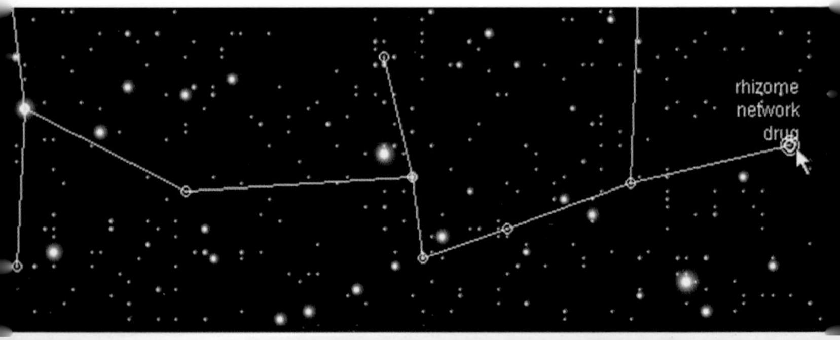

39. Hypertinence

Today's favorite search engine is Google, a system that is so fast and so precise as to raise hopes that one day we will be able to access information on line almost as fast as we do in our own mind. Google presents its search results in order of their relevance and importance rather than in alphabetical order or by date. This is accomplished through a patent-pending technology called PageRank that rates the importance of pages using the "connective intelligence" of the Web. Google interprets a link from Page A to Page B as a "vote" by Page A for Page B. Google assesses a page's importance by the votes it receives. Google also analyzes the page that cast the vote. Votes cast by pages that are by themselves "important" weigh more heavily and help to rate the importance of other pages.

A new breed of search engines allows you to query directly from your document by-passing all the tedious steps of going to the appropriate site and typing the appropriate keyword. With "Gurunet", all you have to do is to Alt-click any word on the screen, and you can access the pertinent information if it's available.

Now that thinking and writing appear on screen and are shared between people, they acquire a new status. Hypertext once again externalizes speech in a formal setting, but this time, the writing is not fixed but fluid and the reading processes are available to others in a collaborative manner. Hypertext is automatically archived, not as a straight recording, as if it were audio or videotaped, but as an articulate database of knowledge that is retrievable in controlled configurations. Non-linear access to the individual items contained in a collaborative exchange allow forms of retrieval that are getting closer to the kind of non-linear access that the mind of a listener has to the meaning created and suggested by a speaker.
Hypertext can thus be structured into potentially durable and retrievable forms of group thinking.

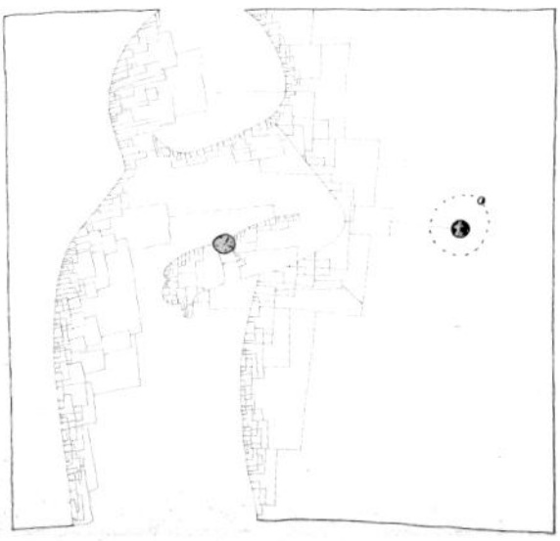

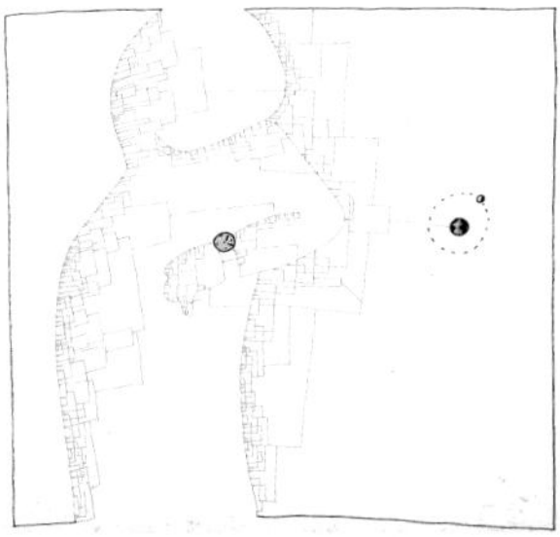

40. Emigration of Mind From Head To Screen

For cyborgs [...] the border between interiority and exteriority is destabilized. Distinctions between self and other are open to reconstruction (William Mitchell, 1995).

The impact of cyberspace on mental space is that whereas mental activities were internalized and privatized by the literate bias, the screen is externalizing them. This began to happen long before the invention of the Internet since the first computers which were already dedicated to a major mental process that is calculation. Computation, a primary function of the brain was to be implemented in computers for many secondary elaborations such as simulating, designing, rendering, morphing, combining, sorting, classifying, storing, retrieving and reorganizing information. The other factor that continues to encourage this externalization process is the shift of dominance from the visual to the tactile.

The difference between perspective and 3-D is as dramatic as the difference between the α and the ε-principles. The dominance of the visual bias in the literate world pushes reality, the world, away from the self, keeping the world at a safe and reasonable distance so to speak. Perspective puts the spectators outside the spectacle, while 3-D drags them back in. Indeed, the world seen from the point of view begins to spread out optically from the surface of the eye outwards. This excludes the body of the spectator from the spectacle. This distancing act has been critical to afford a critical stance to the observer. The contemporary visualizing technique during the Baroque era introduced "trompe-l'oeil" as the conversion of touch into vision, precisely to maintain the distance between the spectator and the spectacle, hence rendering unnecessary the verification by the hand of what was presented to the eye. The insistence of providing a privileged point-of-view to the spectator was to endow people with a greater physical and psychological autonomy, but it also amounted to a kind of "expulsion" from the realm of action to one of theory and contemplation.

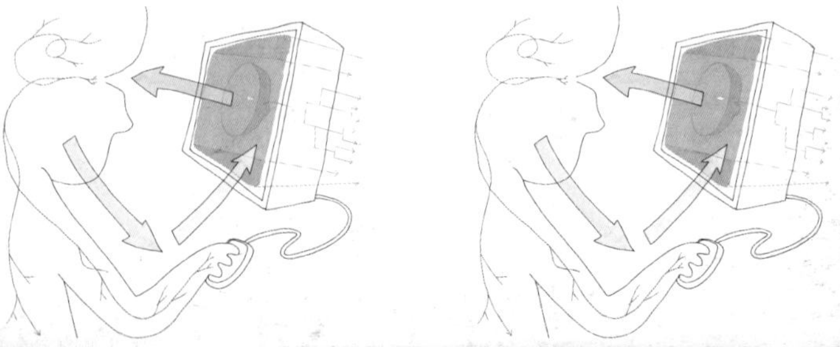

41. E-MERSIVITY

We become true inhabitants of electronically mediated environments rather than mere users of computational devices (William Mitchell, 1999).

Literate people are always inside looking out as if they were always in front of a page, a stage, a painting, a photograph or a film. The exact opposite is true of the user of any form of computer-assisted visual experience, be it 3-D, VR, interactive installation or what have you. Such devices bring the user into the object of vision.

In the Neo-baroque world of radical digitization that we are experiencing now, all the new visualization techniques, VR, holography, 3-D, interactive systems, even morphing and certainly desktop devices, all invite the user back into the spectacle. This spells the "end of theory", namely the end of the safe distance established by the principle of visual dominance between the user and the world. Touching brings you into the world. All the other sensory activities, hearing, tasting and smelling bring the world into you. The user of multimedia is sucked into the world, thus verifying the epistemological reversal implied in the emigration of mind from head to screen. Just as all interactivity is tactile in principle, all interactions are immersive. VR and 3-D puts visual rendering in the service of a total surround tactile experience. Immersion is not merely wearing goggles and datagloves, that is the folkloric end of the spectrum. It is the penetration of the screen itself.

E-mersion and the epistemology of cyberspace
Immersion in dataspace could be renamed "e-mersion" to distinguish it from the other kinds and also to underline the fact that this peculiar form of immersion does not drown those who practice it. Even when they are restricted to the real-time correlation between the pointer and the user, all interactions with the screen are forms of immersion. But the most literal of immersive technologies is what goes under the common name of Virtual Reality, "a computer-generated, interactive, three-dimensional environment in which a person is immersed"[17].

42. Immersivity

AR = VR + R (Augmented Reality is Virtual Reality + Reality)

According to Jenny Holzer, "VR is a technology, medium and concept. It is not three different things, but three different aspects of the same idea, the ability to control and create experience. At present, the term virtual reality refers to seven different ideas and technologies: simulation, interaction, artificiality, immersion, telepresence, full body immersion, and networked communication"[18].

VR is a kind of Objective Imaginary in which people can both command and share experiences that are real but neither really material, nor truly mental. In a Computer-Assisted-Virtual-Environment, a CAVE, people can recover their point-of-view, but they are this time within the environment, not in front of it as with cinema or TV. It is an environment of total surround. The body is the pointer in CAVEs life-size interactivity. On the contrary, the pointer grows into a body of sorts in the AlphaWorlds and other built environment on the web. William Mitchell describes this condition in E-Topia:

> Mark Weiser's ubiquitous computing project of making workers wear "wireless transponder pins that allowed a computer to track their locations [...] The inhabitants became, in effect, living cursors; information that they needed automatically followed them [...] And the building always knew, from moment to moment, exactly where to forward their phone calls and their e-mail[19].

The avatars, which represent the users, have this property that they can either represent them as little digital figures sometime endowed with movements and speech, or as the source of the point-of-view of the user in the world. Epistemologically, this may be one of the most interesting paradoxes of immersivity. The point-of-view becomes also the "point-of-being" in the cyberworld.

> In a virtual world, not just objects but space itself is interactive. As a consequence the virtual environment that surrounds the visitor itself can appear to be something "live" or "animate" (Margaret Morse, 1997).

43. MIND-MACHINE-DIRECT-CONNECT

The relationship to screens via GUIs is the occasion for another great reversal. The axis or vector of information-processing is inverted from the within orientation of the reader to the without orientation of the user in front of a screen. Nothing could account better for the reversal from literate introversion to interactive extroversion that is occurring right now. We can imagine along with cyberphilosopher Michael La Chance that if we combine eye contact and eye-action with any element of our screen, something that is technically feasible today, we could achieve a very close similarity between the way we operate our mind and the way we can thus summon, hold, retain, process, store and combine information in our computer and networked systems. I can readily imagine myself morphing my way from window to window, and from link to link. winking at this icon to get it to link me to the other.

Such a possibility was explored not too long ago by Dirk Lusebrink and Joachim Sauter with their Zerseher installation which allowed the user to change the composition of a painting on a computer screen simply by looking at it (an eye-tracking device followed the gaze of the art patron and correlated it with a hidden cursor which in turn disturbed the order of the pixels that had been gazed upon). Another system called Biomuse rendered the same effect less expensive and more accessible by referencing the muscular movements of the eyes sensed at the level of the user's temples.

Mind-machine-direct-connect may be one of the principles operating in the background of technological development of interfaces. In some military aviation experiments, the mind of the pilot is connected to a computer by sensors comparable to the ones mentioned above, and trained to act as a "third hand" to execute commands. The point is that the connection we entertain with the world's memory could one day be as close as the one we enjoy in the privacy of our mind.

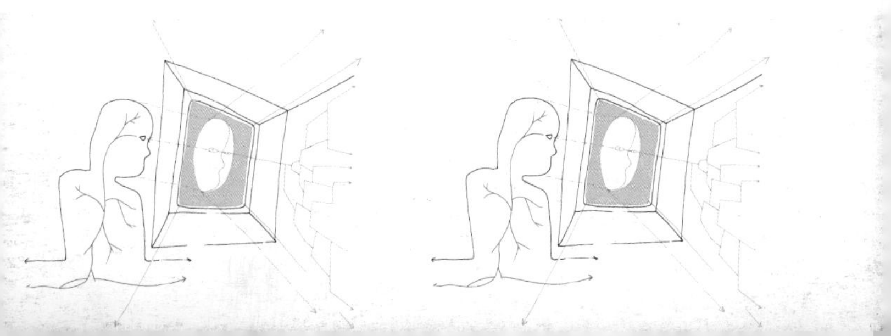

4. The Architecture of Connectivity

44. Epistemological Variability

After modernity, virtuality: all that is solid melts into information. Between modernity and virtuality, transmodernity (Marcos Novak, 1998).

The intelligence of architecture

Galeria Virtual
VR is a 3-D fiction that explores the way people build the contents of their own imagination and how they relate to it. Roc and Narcís Parés y Burghos were among the first artists to exploit Virtual Reality to reveal its epistemological dimension. In the course of stripping down a virtual structure, the user discovers the paradoxical necessity of architecture to be both fluid and solid. As you proceed into the installation, with goggles and pointing device, you are invited to click away all the basic elements of the physical world's infrastructure, color, texture, weight, form, time, down to Descartes' *x,y,z* coordinates, and then nothing, total darkness. At this point you are invited to consider "rebuilding the world" as you deem wisest. *Galeria Virtual* is a metaphor that works at many levels: it symbolizes the attack of the virtual on the real as a pure deconstructing device; it signifies the enormous – but perhaps ultimately illusory – power technology gives to its users; it connects very intimately the world of mind and desire to that of expression and shareable imagination.

3-D Modeler
For a complementary epistemological VR structure, among the most interesting systems developed by the Head Mounted Display Unit at the University of North Carolina at Chapel Hill, under the general direction of Fred Brooks, is the *Virtual 3-D Toolkit or 3-D Modeler*. This is a kind of expanded electronic paint box which allows you to occupy a virtual structure while you are building it, provided, of course, that you are wearing VR goggles. Technically, adding a 3rd dimension to a paint box may seem to be nothing more than just another feature. Conceptually, it is spellbinding because it creates a completely new epistemological condition. It is just as if you were able to physically occupy your own imagination outside your head. It makes the concept of the "objective imaginary" very tangible.

45. Tunneling Memory

Experiments in virtual reality allow artists to explore profound epistemological variations.

Le tunnel
Maurice Benayoun's *Tunnel sous l'Atlantique* allows one to navigate in images of the past tunneled into galleries between a real point of departure, say Paris, and a real point of arrival, in this case, Montreal. The tunnel brings together the real and the virtual and genuinely turns navigation into an exploration of common memory. While digging and unearthing images representing memorabilia of what bound France to Canada in the past, missionaries and armies and rulers and ancient treatises with the First Nations people, you proceed towards a goal, that is to meet someone who, like yourself but from the other side of the ocean, is coming to meet you.

When the connection is made, via a common gallery opened by both diggers at each side, they meet in real-time thanks to an elegantly treated video-conferencing image of the person at the other side. The metaphorical play on traversing the Atlantic, navigating to reach destination, and digging into the past evokes a powerful interpretation of cyberspace, one that presents our collective memory as a living and shared environment.

An even bolder variation on the same principles proposed by Benayoun is the Z-A Profiler, a personal interpreting function added to the system so that while you travel in space and time, it remembers who you are and what you prefer and guides you towards areas of greater pertinence. Without requiring any other input from you than that arising from your behavior in the system, the time you take, the things you look at, the way you look at them, the profiler will sample from an indexed database the elements that will create an environment corresponding to your taste. One application of this system is called *Tunnel des voyages* which facilitates the virtual tourist's selection of pleasurable packages. It is a kind of mild version of Verhoeven's *Total Recall*...

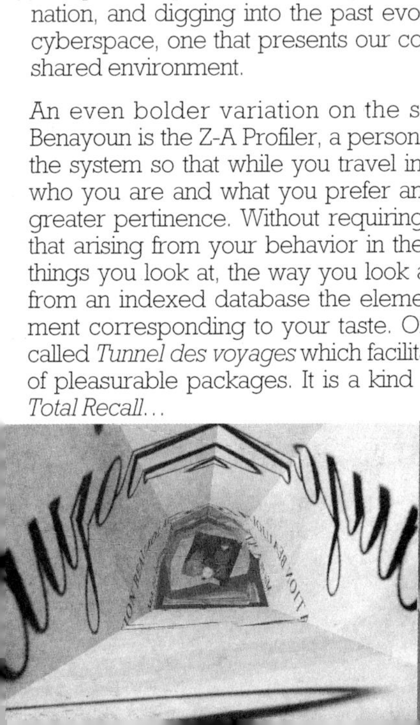

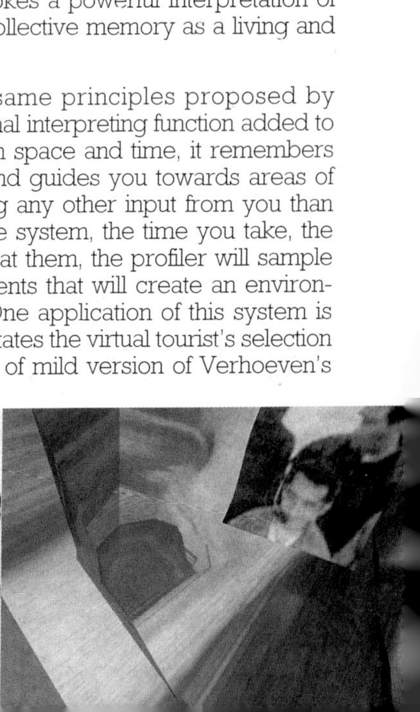

46. Imagineering

"Les fonctions sont dans l'épaisseur des murs, jouent dans les interfaces. L'espace n'est plus un contenant, l'espace est ce qu'en libèrent les parois, il n'est presque plus contingent" (Jean Nouvel).

Osmose

A fourth epistemological fable is provided by Osmose, a profound statement by Char Davies about the artificiality of the digital world and its intimate relationship with the organic reality of our bodies. The new intimacy, and tactility afforded by virtual architectures inspired the use of a breathing sensor to navigate in Osmose. To move up and down the nine levels of the bucolic virtual woods created by Davies, all you need to do, after having donned the appropriate equipment, is to inhale (up) or exhale (down). If you breathe normally, you stay on the same level. You can navigate by pointing or turning your head to look at something in particular. The architectural lesson here is that the surface of the world responds to the body interactively, as opposed to providing a resistance against which the body can exercise its autonomy. Especially impressive in terms of epistemology is the span of experiential levels between the bottom layer (a bewildering array of criss-crossing 0/1 strings) and the top (quotes from famous thinkers and scientists that eventually charted the way to the Virtual).

Technologies of simulation both on and off-line are becoming so flexible, affordable and user-friendly that they eliminate the need for slow and difficult steps in drafting and modeling. They allow faster processing and rendering, hence a closer approximation to thinking. Imagining and imaging almost become one. All simulating machines, like the mind of Prometheus (which means "thinking ahead"), are essentially "projective": they show simulations of things that are not yet actualized, not made. Images on a computer screen, as opposed to video or even "live" TV, are not mere "replays", like photography, but "remakes" of reality. In fact they are the ideal laboratory for ideas and design because they are like imagination itself, free and fluid, but, like the real world, objective, published, shareable.

47. Liquidity

Liquid architecture is not the mimesis of natural fluids in architecture. First and foremost it is a liquidizing of everything that has traditionally been crystalline and solid in architecture. It is the contamination by media (Marcos Novak).

The opportunity for the architect is not merely to improve the drafts or the elevations, or even benefit from the CAD system, it is to rethink the real. How do architects greet this opportunity ?

Like Joyce's Dedalus, Marcos Novak is rethinking the real as if "to forge the uncreated consciousness of his race". As Paolo Portoghesi did before him, Novak wants to name the era. The concept of "Trans-modernity" appears to follow logically upon that of "Post-Modernity". In developing this notion, Novak continues to articulate architecture on the axis of Modernity, but to turn it around so to speak, reversing the vector of personal and social consciousness from the immediate past to an enlarged future. People will begin to think ahead in groups if they are inspired by this concept. The virtual changes the vector of time in the relationship between the actual and the virtual.

It is not clear what contemporary architecture is equivalent to the Centre Pompidou to typify transmodernity and give support to evidence of changes in our relationships to technology. How would one see Frank Gehry or Claude Cardinal, or Santiago Calatrava, or Lars Spuybroek's works in terms of Post-Modernism? They are clearly different. They have in common the breaking of the line, the square and the box, they invite the notion and the perception of flows, orderly in Calatrava, more truly liquid in Gehry, Spuybroek or Oosterhuis.

One could attribute to the effects of CAD and computer-design generally the liberation of the architectural form from the constraints of logic. Novak, however, goes beyond the building altogether, pushing architecture into the realm of communication rather than grounding it in its original "solid state". This approach is emulated by several other architects and thinkers, and especially by what must begin to be known as the "Dutch School" with Lars Spuybroek, Kaas Oosteruis, Van Berkel and Bos, Jan Willem van Kuilenburg, et al.

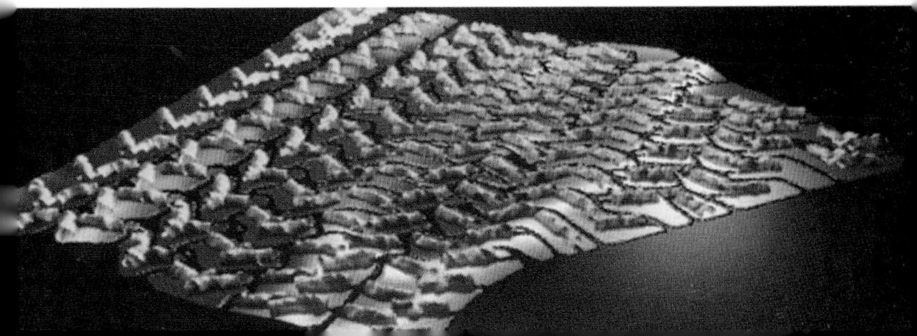

48. Testing Hypersurface

There is no structured information on the outside, it becomes information only by forming itself through my body, by transforming my body, which is called action (H. Maturana and F. Varela, The Tree of Knowledge, Shambala, 1987, ch. 7).

Stephen Perella's notion of "hypersurface" finds itself at the limit between the physical – proprioceptive – and the mental spaces. Hypersurface is the interpretation of the senses by virtuality. When all the senses are reduced to the digital, they mesh into one single moebius-strip like perpetual surface. Even depth is superficial in VR. Everything there is felt even before it is seen. As Lars Spuybroek observes about Tamas Waliczky`s *The Garden*:

> This is not perception but proprioception. Everything immediately becomes networked within the body, where the seen is the touched and the felt, where no distinction can be made between the near and the far, between the hand of manipulation and the sphere of the global (V2, p. 155).

For Spuybroek, time and space are reunited under the control of time: "Space is never a given. There can be space in time, but not the other way around" (idem, p. 138). This is a predictable return to a medieval philosophical position that is the precise opposite from that of Newtonian Physics and Euclidian geometry (where, by the way, we happen to live). In effect, it refutes the infinity of Space to replace it by the infinity of Time. This could also be a new version of the age-old Heraclitean battle between the solid and the liquid, the hard and the soft, a natural occurrence in the era of digitization. Because space is smashed to bits by digitization, it looses both the infinity and perennity that it acquired under the influence of the alphabet.

Spuybroek adds, perhaps reflecting the feeling of many new architects:

> We should even resist thinking in terms of 'space' – I never mention space actually – we have to conceptualize the body first, not the proportional Vitruvian body as the architectural center of the constructed world, no, the experiential body, the excited, vital body, where millions of processes go on at the same time (idem, p. 138).

49. Need for Grounding

Old space has become so tangible it takes physical force to penetrate it…quite literally compared with the cerebral effort of cyberspace (Humberto Maturana).

However, Peter Anders disagrees:

> Space is not a metaphor (!!!) It is a means of thought. Space never loses its validity because it's what the viewer/user brings to the party. Most of our experience is based on spatial understanding - we navigate it, we socialize in it, we draw from it metaphors for more abstract concepts. I have found that arguments for abandoning spatial "metaphors" often favor reducing digital environments to propositional, language-based media. It's wrong-headed, and counter to trends in contemporary computing.

Because computers support near instant gratification to one's conceptual desires, when dealing with cyberspace, there is a temptation to conflate or confound design and reality. C-space and mental space are so close that thinking is becoming in that realm co-extensive with doing. What the floating architecture approach reveals is that electronic media have a tendency to make us lose ground.

> Our knowledge of our being has been grounded in our experience with the actual: with physiology and physics: our bodies and the material space around us. The experience of virtual space confounds that knowledge, by its simultaneous difference and attempts to mask that difference, by trying to seem real yet not quite being so (Carl Francis Disalvo).[20]

The suggestion that the virtual has "liberated" architecture from the constraints of the real baffles even forward thinking architects. In a conversation with Tajima Noriyuki, Tanaka Jun intimates that "gravity-free" design of the kind supported as architecture by Marcos Novak, Greg Lynn and others "is just a kind of utopian idea of architecture as having escaped the limitations of the human body". And he adds, "freedom in architecture can be realized through media as simple as drawing"[21] (TW). Besides, the tendency of "liquid architects" is to concentrate on cyberspace, but there are many other areas of architecture that are concerned.

50. Respecting Thresholds

Connected architecture in physical space

There are several new ways to approach the relationships between the virtual and the actual. To begin, there is hardly any sector of traditional architecture that is not now or will never be affected by networks. Following the telephone lines, these have become almost as ubiquitous in advanced countries as electricity and water. Not only does the building of new schools, hospitals, hotels, museums and galleries and even some cafés require higher installation costs for better wiring and connectivity, but the functions of these places are being modified by the use of networks in their respective contexts. For example, it will become more and more difficult for an educational institution today to avoid considering distance education and its dependence on e-mail, the Web, faxes and, in many cases, videoconferencing. For another example, you will find cyber cafés even in poorly wired areas such as remote parts of India or Africa, because they provide connectivity, a service that the local post office practically always fails to offer, even in advanced countries. *Just* to prove that artists are sometimes way ahead of their time, the first cyber café was created in the early Eighties in Santa Monica by Kit Galloway and Sherrie Rabinowitz, under the name of "Electronic Café". It was and still is based on the combination of Internet and videoconferencing. Its purpose was to renew in telepresence the original vocation of Paris and Amsterdam's 17th century cafés as purveyors of social and political discussion and conversations. One could say that Kit and Sherrie were among the very first people who would qualify as "cybertects".

Access

I found it impossible this year to find a convenient spot to do e-mail at the Frankfurt airport, not even in its sparkling post office. At the Charles De Gaulle airport in Paris, provided you have access to the business class lounge and carry with you the ridiculous French telephone plug, you can get on line. Woe to the traveler in economy anywhere in the airports of the world.

51. Rethinking Building Units

It will soon appear unconscionable that a big city post office and other government institutions such as public libraries and information centers do not also provide public access (for a fee or for free) to e-mail and broad bandwidth.

One wonders what is keeping us waiting. When, almost 30 years ago, the world banking institutions decided to exploit cyberspace – at a time when the term did not yet exist – they found the means to do so. Why is it that today, we do not find access to networked communications to any degree comparable to the ubiquitous presence of Automatic Teller Machines (ATM)? They are the ideal models for providing a necessary threshold between the real and the virtual, dispensing "real money" thanks to a "virtual" transaction. They are user-friendly and offer even complex financial services on minimal bandwidth. These are indeed the main issues of connected architecture in real space: access and bandwidth. Soon, an architect who would present a design for a building that did not include provisions for a cyber infrastructure – read, good wiring and consideration for "the last mile" of connectivity – will look as silly as the one who, back in the early Seventies, built a 20-story apartment building in Arizona, without allowing room for an elevator.

Dedicated areas

Architects and designers are invited to consider new building units and special areas such as media rooms for new needs. They need to be properly integrated within the built structures. Today, hotels anywhere in the world that are not equipped minimally to provide e-mail access to their guests deserve to lose business fast. The better hotel chains are smarting up, but not enough. Yes, there is connectivity in every room, but why not devote a suite to top quality videoconferencing, instead of the jerry rigs the least backward places offer now? Considering the expenses hotel managers go through to equip their conference centers, why is the physical space not available for extended boardroom meetings when the communication technologies already are? The reason is that the people who build hotels do not hire cybertects.

52. Augmenting the Actual

We make our buildings and our buildings make us (Winston Churchill).
Now we make our networks and our networks make us (William Mitchell).

The expanded place

It is obvious that the networks expand the reach of any architectural structure. This factor is already modifying the relationship between head offices and their branches:

> The physical office buildings of a company could be spread across the world, but would at the same time be hooked up to each office in virtual sense to form a digital office. In effect, the whole conglomerate would be present in each of its real locations as an architectonic, organizational, and social unit.[22]

It has become obvious to many commercial enterprises that they can benefit enormously from interconnecting their branch offices or even their suppliers via the Internet. It is what is commonly known as an Intranet. Even museums and galleries are well advised to take advantage of the considerable extension networks can give both to their hoarding capacity and to their reach. Not too long ago, a cybernaut who went under the name of "Service 2000" ran a practical joke on British galleries and museums that were still failing to take advantage of the Web to promote and extend their services. Service 2000 created over 30 websites with URLs either approximating the authentic URLs of galleries with poor sites, or pretending to be the site of those that did not have one. The fake sites were purposely ridiculous and, of course, did not help the cause of their namesake in the eyes of the rising potential cyberclientele. They have now been removed by force of law.

Then again, one wonders about the gallery webmasters who feel the need to repeat the physical experience of the user in cyberspace:

> A "Virtual Museum" in the fullest sense of the term can be constructed as a realistic 3-D model complete with a realistic museum interior and with interactive exhibits to re-create the experience of visiting a museum. As in a real museum, the user can wander through the rooms and corridors in the virtual structure and interact with the exhibits along the way.

53. Redoubling the Actual

Virtual space is not so much space as "nonspace", for it need not occupy ground, nor be a continuous linear extension, area or void, nor even constitute the interval between things (Margaret Morse).

The duplicated space

Blissfully oblivious or perhaps indifferent to the differences involved in the experience, the author Helmut Tichy adds:

> If this 3-D model were available on the Internet, would constructing this museum be redundant? In contrast to an actual exhibition, the users could have access 24 hours/7 days a week to the virtual exhibition from anywhere in the world via an Internet connection. Therefore, virtual museums could be visited simultaneously by anyone, not just by people in its vicinity.

Once again, in this comment, we find the rampant "substitution bias" as if the possibilities afforded by one medium automatically called for the elimination of the previous media. This is far from the case with exhibit areas. Not only do people's taste for the "real thing" augment with their virtualization as Walter Benjamin observed a long time ago, but the principle of necessary materiality is best expressed in the combination of a real museum and its virtual extension. What the new medium does, as McLuhan often observed, is to convert the previous medium into an art form. Hardware galleries and museums are rethinking themselves earnestly under the pressure of digitization. The need to duplicate the real thing walls and all, however, may not be so pressing for all museums and galleries on line. There are a dozen examples of cyberspatial extensions of museums that do not feel the need to duplicate digitally and can still provide superlative services. *The Smithsonian Without Walls* by Plumbdesign is a case in point. This magnificent site shows the potential for combining real, virtual and mental spaces as an extension to the museum.

The real need to duplicate a space is when the image is used either to help navigation in a very real sense or when, as in the case of an early quicktime VR application developed at the McLuhan Program, Graham Smith planned the galleries of a dam to help monitor the pressure cracks in their supporting walls.

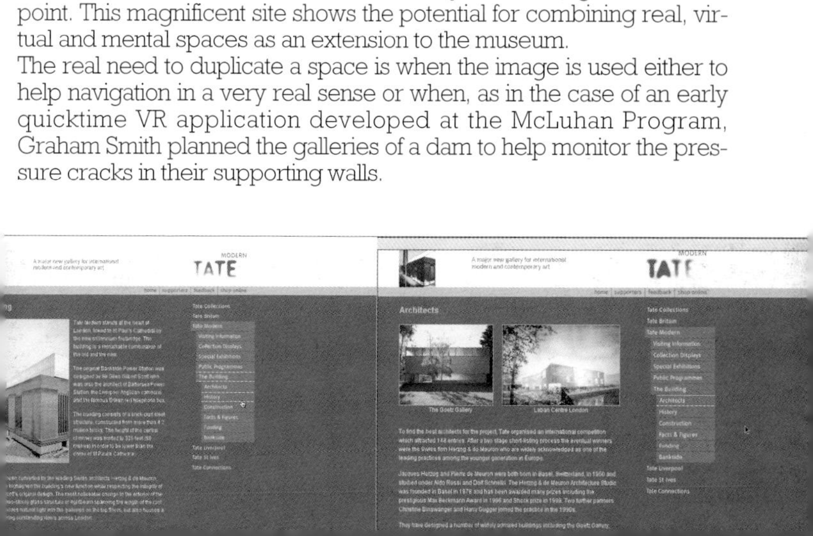

54. Digitizing the City

I am trying to think about the relation between the corporeal and empirical elements of (physical) architecture and cities, and (metaphysical) architecture as knowledge or thought (Tajima Noriyuki, 1998).

Of all these solutions searching for a problem, the most promising is T-Vision. T-Vision is a navigation tool of the first order which allows full access to cyberspace and which is focused on Berlin because that is where Art + Com, its developers, reside. T-Vision allows one to circulate in virtual representations of Berlin's streets and buildings. However, except for the visibly superior quality of the design and the closer definition of the landscape and buildings, that in itself would not rate much higher than other digital cities for usability. But Art + Com is doing something else. It is digitizing and integrating in a scalable way all the photographic and filmic material that documents Berlin's past and thus allows the Cybernaut to surf in Berlin's past as well as its present. Suddenly, the real city, virtualized as a support for the precise location of memory becomes a much more viable metaphor. Presently, Art + Com is experimenting with automated 3-D rendering to give depth and freedom of point-of-view to these old photographs and films. Berlin hence, is a good place to see the enmeshment between mental space, with its powerful management of symbols, physical space in its uncanny reliability, and cyberspace that binds both ubiquitously. Again, a pertinent idea of Tanaka illuminates the question:

> In the city as a site of memory, you would remember things as spatial representations in your head and then place an item that you wanted to remember in a particular place. So the city itself was the site and system of memory – a place where memories could be internalized through the reading of these sites. As the system of memory itself shifts into cyberspace, the organization of the archives and the control of memory will become less and less spatial. Thus precisely because the metaphor of space has lost its validity we are faced with an even greater need for cyberspace design (*op. cit.*, p. 82).

55. Worldmaking

Hi handsome ! Are you new in town ?
No, I'm the same, the town has changed (from the movie *Choose Me*).

Architecture in cyberspace
Beside cities that duplicate and extend real ones such as Digital Toronto, Digitale Stad and Cyber Berlin, there are several categories among what one might call "pure" cyber-urban architectures, that is buildings and cities that are fictional and entirely contained in cyberspace: game-cities like Simcity that are built by a single user, just for the fun of it, or as a learning tool for urban planning; cybercities like Alphaworlds to which many people contribute and that support communities at different levels of role-playing.

The publication of *Snow Crash* (1992), a novel by Neal Stephenson, prefiguring the networked "worlds" that are now current, preceded the actual development of cybercities on line by only a couple of years, but it continues to exercise a decisive influence on those who create them.

> Like any place in Reality, the Street is subject to development. Developers can build their own small streets feeding off the main one. They can build buildings, parks, signs, as well as things that do not exist in Reality, such as vast hovering overhead light shows and special neighborhoods where the rules of three-dimensional spacetime are ignored[23].

Marcos Novak and others have correctly observed that cyberspace offers the opportunity to give an objective shape to the contents of one's architectural imagination. Building cities on line, whether they be of the "Simcity" or the Alphaworlds variety is reminiscent of that blissful period when, as children, we used to build cities with the mechanical toys of the times, Dinky toys, Legoland, Tinker toys, Meccano, Marklin train stations and a host of other tools for the imagination of the industrial era. In Jean Piaget's still revered theory of child development psychology, the imagination of space is supported by precisely such activities and is one of the key elements of mental growth. The child learns to control his or her environment by building cities.

56. Translating Metaphors Digitally

– Are you in the middle of nowhere?
– No, but I can see it from here. (From the movie *Thelma and Louise*).

Likewise cybernauts build cities and houses and meeting places in cyberspace because these are metaphors we can all understand. These shapes give instant meaning to the newcomer in cyberspace. The new environment is already suffused with the vocabulary of architecture. Chat rooms, gates, portals, windows, as well as the concepts of digital cities and information highways spell the reign of the metaphorical process that consists in introducing the new through words that contain features of the old. However, because once they appear on screens, these concepts are not mere words, but also designs, they take a stronger hold on our imagination.

This metaphorizing has many uses, as media art curator Reinhardt W. Wolf points out:

> A primary factor is the geographical anchorage: the Digitale Stad in the Netherlands, for instance, addresses primarily the inhabitants of Amsterdam, while the Internationale Stadt (IS) targeted Berliners. [...] A second reason for deploying the metaphor lies in the efficiency of the urban model as an aid to orientation in data space[24].

However, Wolf goes on to say that while cybercities began as social experiments supported by romantic idealizations of the perfect city recovered, the first ones either failed because of lack of participation like Internationale Stadt which lasted less than three years, or were sold to commercial interests like Digitale Stad. Lack of participation is indeed a problem for many cities on line. The reason must be that beyond the cognitive satisfaction of having realized an attractive structure, there is not much use for it.

Under the direction of Bruce Damer, a prominent promoter of Alphaworlds and the author of *Avatars!* a cult book among worlds afficionados, and with the help of people in different parts of the world, we built what we think was the first virtual university in an Active World. It is still there in Sherwood Towne and it has even inspired an international competition for the 3-D modeling of universities.

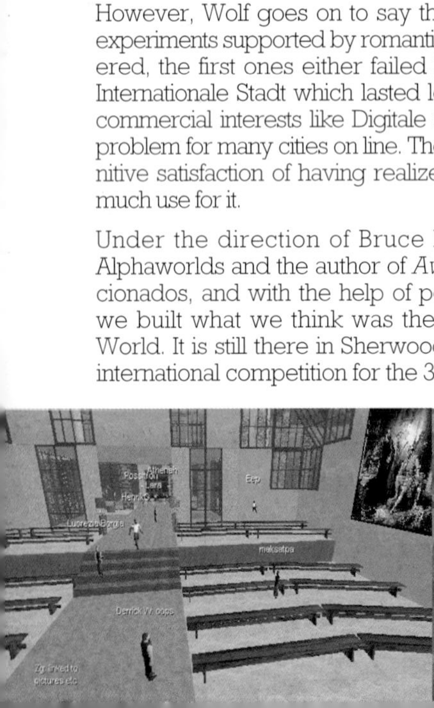

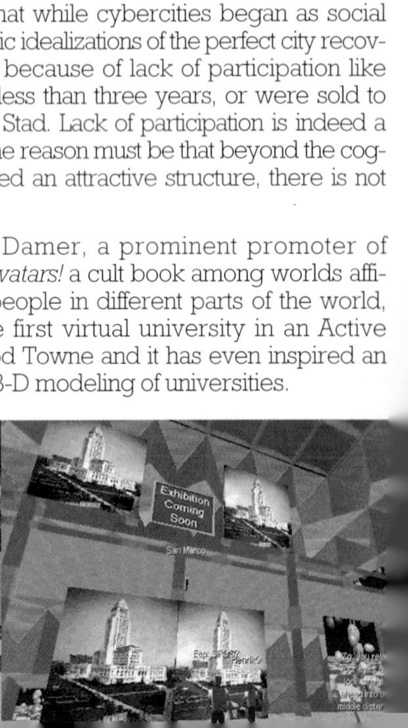

57. Need to have a Reason to go there

As long as there is nothing to guarantee a one-to-one correspondence of these various split bodies, it will be impossible to have a "common space" within the cyber community (Tanaka Jun, 1998).

The U, as it was called, attracted many visitors in the first few days, but whenever I would call it up to show it at conferences, there was nobody there. I stopped showing it. I guess people go to universities to take courses and none being offered at *The U* that somehow explains the lack of visitors. Still, my experience with 3-D environments on line has been that there are few occupants at any one time. Tanaka may have one answer to this lack of attachment to cyber cities:

> It is certainly no longer effective simply to replace real space by virtual space. This is because the double layering of subjectivity and transcendent perspective has ceased to function inside cyberspace – something which is related to the impossibility of identifying the self on the Internet [...] this is related to the structural difficulty of occupying a transcendent perspective in order to establish the identity of any given thing.

There are cybertectural conditions for this paradoxical materialization of architectural dreams to be effective. Building a 3-D city on line is not in itself such a great accomplishment. In many schools of the world this kind of exercise has become a classroom assignment. As Borre Ludvigsen observes:

> It is infinitely easier and more expedient to create the architecture of fictional cyberspace than it is to give the matrix of cyberspace meaningful form. The various standards and guidelines available today do not form a coherent architectural politic. While the human interface guidelines of various graphical user interfaces (GUIs) apply themselves to what results in architecture, they do not relate to each other or the underlying technologies by their intent to form "emotional relationships". Nor do they attempt to answer the functions of interrelated technologies. Such attentions when they do arise come about through external techno-economic pressures affected more by the health of stocks and shares than the needs of order and planning.[25]

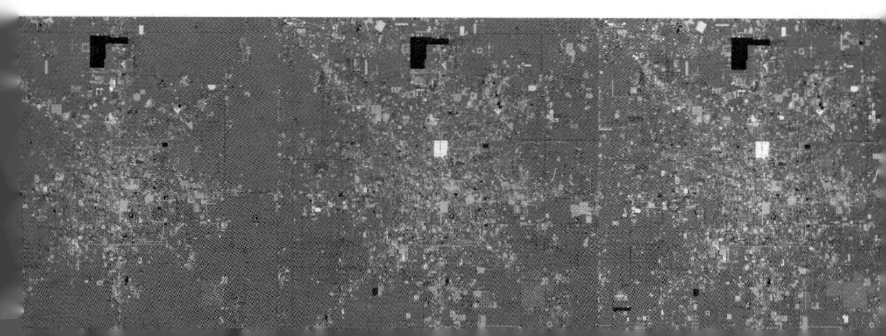

58. Mixing the Actual and the Virtual

There are also ways to introduce the virtual into the actual, or vice-versa. Monika Fleischmann and Wolfgang Strauss, who is an architect by profession, have helped to introduce the concept of mixed reality by creating media tools and environments that bring the virtual into the actual and vice-versa so as to enhance collaboration and communication. One architectural idea is to find the way to interconnect people at a distance so as to provide them with a common platform or structure where each user occupies a position and effects commands corresponding to those occupied and performed locally. Their project eMUSE (electronic multi-user stage environment) "links real and virtual space in a mixed-reality shared environment for group interaction around common data. It is realized as a VRML-based networked multi-user environment by means of opening the otherwise closed VRML browser. eMUSE is built as a modular system providing independent levels of implementation for interfacing, rendering and displaying the virtual environment".

The earlier versions of eMUSE were dependent on studio-based calibration. A further elaboration, Netzspannung, pushes the project to a more open, less technology heavy, public utility kind of set-up. Created to stimulate the art community, Netzspannung is an extendable Internet platform geared specifically towards cooperation and shaping by the community. The users provide the contents, but also define the modes of their interactions in the common platform. Netzspannung is based on what Fleischmann and Strauss call a Distributed Community Engine (DCE):

> The separation of interface, application and database layers enables the deployment of multiple independent database and application servers, as well as decentralized and managed interfaces. Each user can run his/her own server with their own set of functionalities.

Deep down, Netzspannung is an architecture of collaboration, that is, an architecture of intelligence.

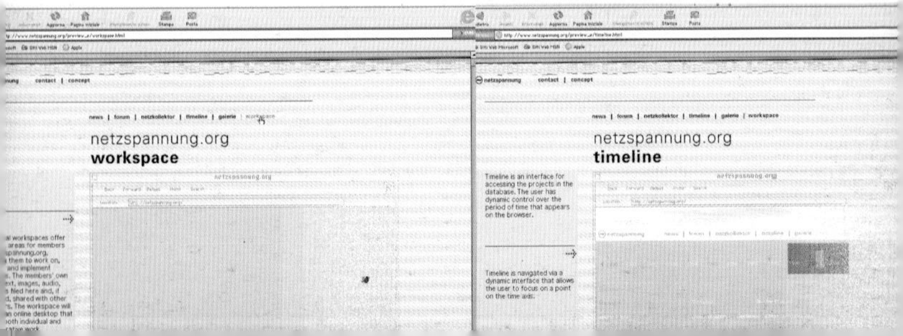

59. Skins: Integrating Actual and Virtual

> *Architecture as the epidermis must be pliant and supple like our skin and be able to exchange information with the outside world. Architecture clad in such a membrane should instead be called a media suit* (Toyo Ito, 1994).

The building of thresholds between real and cyberspace obviously evokes a generous array of new formulas. Artists are working out the news tools for the interaction. Consider the intriguing project by Rafael Lozano-Hemmer, *Displaced Emperors*, an outdoors art installation permitting people to explore, in a city-size hypertext, various aspects of the history of the settings and of the occupants, by projecting them at appropriate places on the walls of the monuments in question. The whole idea is to cover the real buildings with layers of digital skins that tell their story. This, of course, is even simpler to realize on line than in physical space. This kind of work is in cultural resonance with a new tool called "skin", a software application that can "dress up" the digital part of information appliances. It is also in line with a much older skin, that of the neon signs of advertising covering the commercial facades of our cities.

Interactive plant growing

The idea of "extended skin" can also be explored in a body-based rather than building-based sensitivity. Interior decorators might find fresh inspiration from *Interactive Plant Growing*, an interactive art installation by Christa Sommerer and Laurent Mignonneau presented at *Ars Electronica* in Linz in 1993. By approaching and lightly touching an array of plants, you cause an offshoot of a digital replica of the plant to grow on a screen wall behind it. The real plant has a sensing device attached to its stem and every contact, even mere proximity will create a reaction. I immediately imagined that this kind of sensor device could be used to create sensitive walls, responsive to the mood of the occupants, or interacting with them by selecting music to soothe their spirits.

The skin is the hypersurface, par excellence. Let us not forget here that the skin is a tactile part of the body, not only something to look at, but also one of the most comprehensive systems of sensors that the body can boast of. And, of course, the skin is electric. Since Toyo Ito and Jean Nouvel have pointed the way, architects have begun to pick up on the notion of skin.

60. Networking the Skin

In 1996, I met Christian Moeller to interview him for a series of television shows I was doing for TVOntario, an educational television outfit in Canada. Impressed by his many explorations of interactivity and virtuality, I naturally imagined him to be an "artist" and I told him so. To which he replied to my surprise: "I am not an artist, I am an architect". I didn't get it then, considering the value of being a world class artist every bit as significant as being a good architect, if not more so. Now I can see that the boundaries between art, design and architecture are loose and shifting. Several installations by Moeller involve the notion of "skins", including *Networked Skin* that he and Joachim Sauter developed for the Ars Electronica Centre in Linz, Austria:

> The surface of the two-story facade that runs around the building is constructed of large translucent glass panels. By day the facade appears as an opaque decorative wall of greenish-white glass. In the evening and at night the opaque glass surface functions as a projection screen. All computer users connected to global networks are invited via Internet news services or email to send picture files over the Net to the AEC. The AEC computer network receives and sorts these files. The pictures are then projected according to their geographical origin onto a "virtual globe". Both static and moving pictures are projected onto "virtual billboards" arranged vertically to the virtual globe. These billboards turn to face the viewer, whether they are approached from above or walked past. As moving picture sequences can also contain sound, a tonal dimension is created as more and more sequences start up. As individual objects are approached, their individual sound levels can be distinguished. The images can be moved with the aid of a globe set into the ground that functions like a trackball and is called *Earthtracker*. The latter functions as an interface for visitors to navigate through this virtual world. By turning the Earthtracker, they can control the speed and direction of their virtual movements. In addition, by means of a bar which resembles a latitude scale, they can alter both the elevation (by pushing the bar up or down) and the direction (by turning the bar) of their movements.

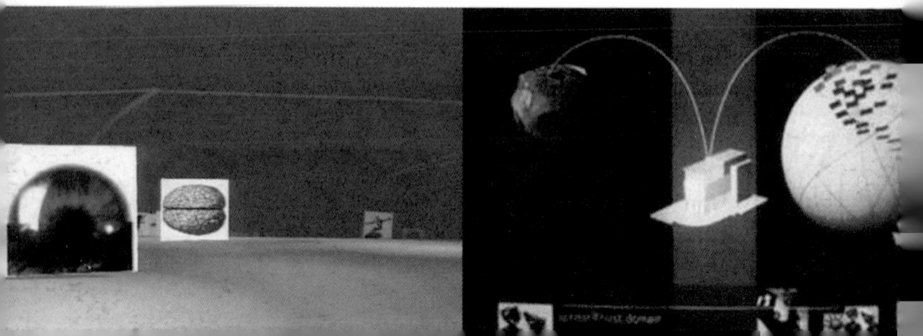

61. City Skin

Architecture is our collective epidermis, dressed roughly as a blacksmith, or in the haute couture of the moment (Ted Krueger, 1996).

A quasi-literal interpretation of the principle of "skin" extended to the whole city is MONO LAB's computer-assisted re-thinking of both the landscapes and the cityscapes of several venerable Dutch cities. To extend the open, livable space now retreating before the invasion of sprawling habitat, and to restore landscapes to the cityscape, MONO LAB proposes projects to allow synthesis of urban program, landscape and infrastructure by mediating membranes. These would be built in such a fashion to allow sufficient light and air and provide access routes and services in a smooth and elegant way. The power of the skin metaphor is that it does invite reconsidering space occupancy in radically new ways. As bold as it looks, the design is not a fantasy. It's another one of these wild Dutch experiments. Some urban planners are thinking along these lines. For example, a plan has been recently proposed in Toronto to grow grass on the roofs of the city to lower the greenhouse effect of the sunlight reflecting on concrete.

In another vein on the topic of skins, the architect Toyo Ito's often-repeated suggestion – inspired by McLuhan – that architecture should emulate our skin and become pliant and sensitive brings a logical conclusion to a trend in design and architecture towards the etherealization of the interface. Ito's suggestion brings the history of the wall to the point where it disappears into thin air. If one played the history of architecture along the lines Northrop Frye followed to study the human image in literature in *The Anatomy of Criticism*, showing that the heroes of literature never ceased to shrink in size and stature from the legendary characters of early myths to Samuel Beckett's subhuman, we would see that the earliest walls were huge and deep and the latest thin and membrane-like. The size and volume of our lodgings have shrunk from the gigantic Roman proportions to little above the height of the man in the street. The next step is architecture turning into tailoring.

1997 © MONO LAB ARCHITECTS - Infrabody 'Rotte-Delta' - parallel soils with 'Randstad-cowboy'.

62. Relational Architecture

Space in cyberspace is purely relational (both geometrically and socially) (Dodge and Kitchin, 2001).

Often the most challenging, the use of networked architecture to create communities and relationships is growing rapidly. Rafael Lozano-Hemmer has named "relational architecture", architecture that is based not only on topology, but also on making use of media to connect people to buildings and spaces in a configured relationship:

> In relational architecture, buildings are activated so that the input of the people in the street can provide narrative implications apart from those envisioned by the architects, developers or dwellers. The pieces use sensors, networks and audiovisual technologies to transform the buildings.

Alzado Vectorial

Among the most impressive applications of this concept is *Alzado Vectorial*. From anywhere in the world, via the Internet, people are invited to create the design for the pattern of projector beams over the Zócalo Square of Mexico City. To do this, they enter various parameters following simple instructions on a web site. This selection generates commands that automatically sequence and coordinate the projections. "In particular, light projections are used since they can achieve the desired monumental scale, can be changed in real time, and their immateriality makes their deployment more logistically feasible" (Rafael Lozano-Hemmer, *Interview with Geert Lovink*, *Vectorial Elevation*, Conaculta Ed., Mexico 2000, p. 55).

The effect is a light show, but the cause is an architecture of connectivity. Rafael Lozano-Hemmer's approach falls into the ephemeral, instant architecture, entirely based on networks from conception to realization and sustenance. *Alzado Vectorial* is an instant space. The results are spectacular and also metaphorical. They provide us with a radically new understanding of an esthetics of networks proper. The projected patterns are creating an epiphany-making manifest in a visible mode from the coherence and beauty of invisible connections across the planet.

63. Combining Retinal Memory

One of Maurice Benayoun's latest and most striking works explores the relational architecture of the public gaze on the Internet. *Art Impact, Collective Retinal Memory* leads the cybernaut to the total surround rendering of a gallery site in Avignon. As you explore various parts of the display on line, focusing on this detail and zooming on that one or moving from room to room, your visual itinerary and all the objects of your gaze are recorded and stored in the site's temporary data-hold. You can then click on a button to get a composite image your visual itinerary and all the objects of your gaze combined with that of other cybernauts who have preceded you in the space or who were looking at the same time as yourself. The results are both startling and pleasing, but again, it is the psychotectural implication of the piece which strikes the imagination. Benayoun creates and explores new intermediate domains of the objective imaginary, just as novelists of the past since Greco-Roman times have labored to furnish our subjective imagination and have provided us with experiences that we would never have achieved by ourselves.

The point is that these artists' installations are profoundly cybertectural, bringing the real, the virtual and the mental together not merely for effect, but for the promise of enormous substance in the near future. This is the nascent art of cyberspace that reveals both the implications of the new spatial environment for architectural considerations and its connections with the real world, for the integration of past and present. These installations show the way to other cybertects, but also to historians and archivists who might be tempted to combine their resources to create, by similar means, a kind of total environment of memory, taking advantage of the most painstaking research and documentation already available in the libraries and databases of the world, so as to provide instant education. Let us remember that remembering means to re-member, that it is a process of integration that brings separate pieces together again.

5. Principles of Connected Architecture

64. Piloting

> *The Internet is among the greatest architecture the world has ever known, far greater than the material reference point of the information highway metaphor, the freeway system* (Margaret Morse, 1977).

The architecture of intelligence involves the joint management of physical, mental and virtual spaces, but a proper understanding of where and how they interact should prevail. Tanaka Jun's opinion on this subject is enlightening:

> If cyberarchitecture were merely a program which used the computer as a tool, all we would have to do would be to ask whether or not the program was suitable. But the problem is that the technology that we are referring to as cyberarchitecture is also connected to the construction of a space which has become indispensable to us – and as long as this is the case we have to give serious thought to how that space should be designed. I'm not sure whether this is the job for the architect or for the specialist in information-processing, but we also have to ask how to design a new spatiality for the body as interface[26].

Connected architecture

The management of such a new condition calls for new thinking and perhaps a new profession, that of the "cybertect". The etymology of "architect" reveals that the word is made up of two Greek concepts, APXH, the "first" or the "chief" and TEKTON, the "carpenter" or the "builder". The first architects were "master builders". By replacing "archi" by "cyber", the word for "rudder", we keep the building element, but add the new realm of interactive navigation to the function. The cybertect's job is to create reliable pathways and useful environments in cyberspace and between cyberspace and real space. The words "connected architecture" are compelling to me because they bring the two realms together and define the area of specialization that is required to deal formally with them together.

To the extent that architecture deals with building places for people in face-to-face presence, connected architecture deals with structuring connections, designing forms and patterns of telepresence and collaboration in the networks between such places.

While formal architecture was the response to space expanding in perspective, connected architecture is the response to the electronic implosion of space, time and architecture. "As a result", says Tanaka, "you have a convergence of the design of information space with that of real space through the mediation of computer technology".

65. Cybertecture

We are entering an era of electronically extended bodies living at intersection points of the physical and virtual worlds... (William Mitchell, 1995).
The link between analogue and digital fields, concerning to the relationship between architecture and virtual media, demands new functional and typological concepts (Ortlos Architects, 2001).

Connected architecture must address three areas of expertise:
– the thresholds and connections between real and virtual spaces
– the construction of usable virtual environments in cyberspace whether in CAD, VR, CAVEs, VRML, Active Worlds, or any other technology as it appears on the market
-the architecture of connected mental space to the extent that connective cognition now requires the use of cyberspace to be shared in new ways.

A cybertect would need to include considerations about how people will relate not only to the built environments that are created for them in the connections between real and virtual spaces, but also to each other within a predominantly cognitive world. The primary goals of connected architecture, similar to those of Vitruvian architecture, should be to construct useful, reliable and attractive social and cognitive environments.

Brian Thomas Carroll who is the editor of *architexturez.com*, perhaps the best site for basic texts and discussion about connected architecture, is passionate about the reeducation of architecture to include electricity and networks as a matter of prime consideration. The fact is that, without benefiting from formal training in cyberspatial skills, many architects are learning on the job and proposing their sets of principles as guidelines. Here follow some of the main ones, in no particular order of relevance (in fact, all are pertinent simultaneously).

William Mitchell, for example, has developed a set of five principles for what he has named "e-topias", that is lean, green cities that work smarter, not harder: Dematerialization, Demobilization, Mass customization, Intelligent operation, Soft transformation. "We can apply them at the scales of product design, architecture, urban design and planning, and regional, national, and global strategy".

66. MATERIALITY

1. *Dematerialization*: "Replacement of big, physical things by miniaturized equivalents [...] accomplishes much the same result" (e.g. letter replaced by e-mail because it does not consume paper; or heavy copper cables replaced by hair-thin fiber optic, etc.). This principle reflects Nicholas Negroponte's famous "atoms to bits" principle.

2. *Demobilization*: "In general, moving bits is immeasurably more efficient than moving people and goods" (e.g. working from home, downloading film rather than going to the store, and digital distribution generally).

3. *Mass customization*: "We can employ silicon and software on a vast scale to enable automatic custom delivery of just what is required in particular contexts, and no more" (e.g., personalized newspaper, automated updating and delivery of groceries and other domestic goods, electronic management of car rental, etc.).

4. *Intelligent operation*: "By putting more intelligence into devices and systems that require these resources [water, fuel and electric power],we can minimize waste and can introduce dynamic pricing strategies that effectively manage demand and encourage thriftiness" (e.g., intelligent irrigation system, electric sensor system for turning on lights, opening doors, etc.).

5. *Soft transformation*: "In most developed areas... the primary task will be one of adapting existing building stock, public spaces, and transportation infrastructure to meet requirements that are very different from those that guided their initial production"[27].

On the other hand, there is no virtual without actual support for it. For the moment, cyberspace simply can't do without electricity. "The only problem is that architectural students, professors, researchers, theorists, professional architects and, importantly, lay people including patrons, have yet to think electricity is in any way related to the discipline of architecture" (Brian Thomas Caroll).

67. Utility

The principle of Materiality goes well beyond that observation. It stresses the value of anchoring the virtual in the actual, especially where communities and services are concerned. The virtualization of many human activities brings up a countervailing need for grounding in the actual. Connectivity works best in face-to-face interactions, simply because heads and bodies are still the best available information-processing devices.

In terms of a connective project, the anchoring device is the quality and durability of the project that creates the associations. In a sense everything the network does leads to building a community, a "just-in-time" kind of community (which doesn't mean that it is necessarily less durable than many face-to-face ones).

For her part, Anna Cicognani has analyzed the similarities and differences between on-line and off-line architecture and has identified four basic elements that need attention: Matter, Coherence, Speed and Control. She points out that even if the laws of physics only apply to physical matter, it is indispensable to treat the rules of operation of protocols with the same rigor: "When designing, the fundamental rule for dealing with matter is the same, for both physical and on-line environments: respect the nature of the material". This means knowing the functionalities of any given software and making consistent use of its capabilities.

Similarly, regarding coherence, she points out that on-line environments need to make sense to the same extent as off-line ones: "The metaphorical coherence of an on-line environment is fundamental for its utility and flexibility". This implies that, for example, when designing a website for a bank or for a university, the laws of gravity and the resistance of materials may not apply, but spatial orientation and the appropriateness of the kinds of services specific to the industries concerned do apply.

68. Reliability

La maison, qui était primitivement destinée à protéger des intempéries climatiques, est aujourd'hui perméable aux intempéries psychiques (Sylvain Dubuisson).

Indeed, after Vitruvius, we may not need to emphasize the obvious, but what we create in cyberspace needs to make sense to the same extent as in physical or mental spaces. This entails subsets of principles, including hypertinence (which, like the brain, combines maximum speed with maximum precision), reliability, the equivalent of Vitruvius' Firmitas, and Simplicity. In another range of considerations, since, just like the mind, cyberspace is made up essentially of information, to be useful, an object of connected architecture ought to be storable, archivable, retrievable, searchable, analyzable, updatable, modifiable, etc.

Finally, another sense of Utility is the one that makes up the meaning of "utilities". Architecture may one day be obliged to include the virtual and its various networks as a common utility.

The principle of Reliability is taken for granted by all, but, of course, as any user of any version of Windows knows, it shouldn't be. It applies in several ways: the system that is used, whether hardware or software, must be resistant not only to the elements, but also to human malice, be it fraud, misuse or viral propagation. For the mammoth technological takeover to continue, the networks and the software have to be reliable (if only to allow us to retain our private and collective sanity). If, collectively, we do not begin soon to master the protection of the networks and the guaranteed trouble-free functioning of both hardware and software, we will develop epidemics of new neural diseases caused by psycho-sensorial abuse of our CNS by our own contraptions. The problem is acute. The effects of down-time are crippling in a quasi biological manner. Our dependence on regular and trouble-free access to networked communications has taken the proportions of a drug-dependence except that it is both legitimate and necessary.

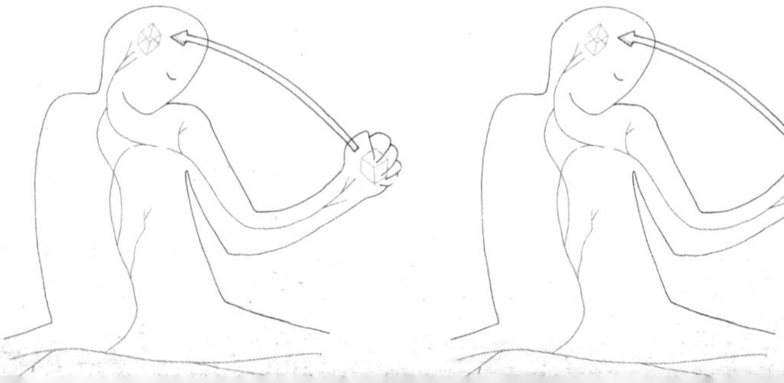

69. Simplicity

A language which uses fewer basic elements to achieve the same power is simpler. Sometimes simplicity is confused with 'easy to understand' (Tim Berners-Lee, 1998-99).

A cyberspatial architecture needs also to be updatable, not to say smoothly modular. At another level, it must resist obsolescence and technological death (as so many early floppy disks that are now unreadable because their supporting hardware is nowhere to be found anymore).

If Vitruvius came back and was given time to ponder the implications of cyberspace, he might approve master cybertect, Tim Berners-Lee's four basic principles: Simplicity, Modularity, Tolerance and Decentralization. Simplicity includes, of course, user-friendliness and conviviality. A contemporary triad of principles equivalent to the Vitruvian three was proposed by Nortel Networks executives at a workshop organized in Boston in October 2000. The concepts under examination included Simplicity along with Ubiquity and Fidelity. Simplicity includes, of course, user-friendliness and conviviality.

Thomas Horan, author of *Digital Places: Building Our City of Bits*, offers five key principles for consideration in the design of successful digital places:

> 1. Designing for multiplicity, which refers to the need for place design to address today's spatial fluidity, which allows people to perform day-to-day activities anytime, anywhere. 2. Designing with traditional place, which embodies the need to design digital places in a manner that respects the value of traditional places such as homes, libraries and schools.
> 3. Designing across architectures, which focuses on the synergistic relationship between electronic exchange (such as e-commerce) and physical exchange (such as bricks-and-mortar stores).
> 4. Designing for community, which stresses the opportunity to connect various civic networks electronically and physically.
> 5. Designing in collaboration, which highlights the need to include a wide range of users in the creation of new high-tech environments.[28]

70. Interactivity

Computer generated worlds are actually much more "haptic" and "aggregate" than "optic" and "systematic" (Lev Manovich, 1996).

Interactivity is the tactile dimension of cyberspace. It gives it pressure, texture and density, as each interfacing tool is a variation of touch, even if it consists in a mere glance at an active button. There is something deeply proprioceptive in our relationship with technology. One of the requirements entailed by Interactivity should most certainly be real-time response and the other, control.

Anna Cicognani addresses both: regarding the issue of Speed, the third of her four basic elements, she evidently stresses the need to achieve as close to real-time a response as possible. But she also underlines the fact that the user can not only obtain a service, but custom design the process itself:

> The capacity to modify an on-line environment is related to the capacity of using interface tools and to the environment responsiveness to their use. The execution of a command is almost immediate, related to the speed of the machine; thus, its output is immediately "visible" to a user. The feedback speed over decisions is an important aspect of design: in online worlds, designers can watch the effects of their actions in a relatively short period of time, compared to design actions performed in the physical world.

Furthermore, to support the basic principle of control, Cicognani brings out a critical element of design that concerns the integrity of the built environments on-line.

> Control on-line is exercised by ownership and access. Each item has an owner, and only that owner, or a system administrator, can modify or destroy it. The digital ownership of entities is much easier to organize and control in the on-line world, rather than in the physical world. The designer's control is a powerful instrument that can restrict the use of the environment to determined classes of users. Even the political and social organization of the on-line environment, which is directly related to access, becomes a design task.[29]

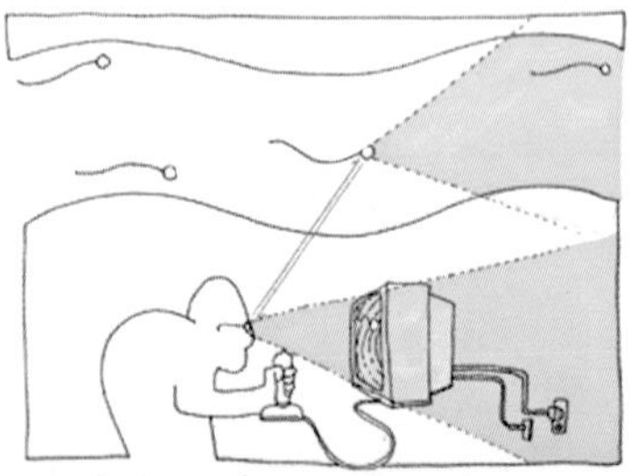

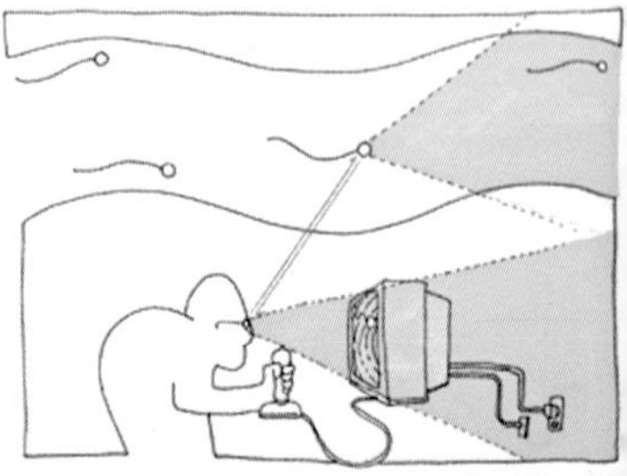

71. Connectivity

Connectivity can, in this context, mean different things: the combination of functionalities; the collapse and opening up in a moment of conflict or rupture; or diversion and repulsion where no interaction can take place (Knowbotic Research Foundation, 1996).

Connectivity is based on maximum access for maximum pertinence. This entails the structuring of every possible form of human associations, many as yet unimagined. So far, the interplay of self-organization and the laws of pertinence seem to have established the checks and barriers to ensure both flow and precision in the networks, but questions of structure will be raised eventually.

Indeed a fundamental issue concerns who should control the basic architecture of the Internet. The two opposing philosophies of private control or public management of globally used operating systems have been expressed elegantly by Eric S. Raymond's comparison between *The Cathedral and the Bazaar* in an essay that is now a standard reference for programmers and philosophers of the Web. Raymond's image of the cathedral is different from that proposed by Margaret Morse. She, like Erwin Panofsky's view of the cathedral, sees it as the product of generations of anonymous builders. Raymond sees it as a centralized operation that benefits all by imposing a single standard. Both are right. Raymond says that, at first, he used to believe in the cathedral model. Launching a Linux-based open-source project called "fetchmail" which succeeded brilliantly against all expectations persuaded him otherwise. Hackers and programmers from everywhere began to use, debug and improve the software. Says Raymond: "The Linux community seems to resemble a great babbling bazaar of different agendas and approaches...out of which a coherent and stable system could seemingly emerge only by a succession of miracles". Raymond's – and Linux – approach most evidently reveals "connected intelligence" in practice, a notion that Raymond translates by: "Given enough eyeballs, all bugs are shallow"[30]. All networks connect intelligences, but those that are built by their users and work to benefit all evidence a new evolutionary degree of both connectivity and intelligence.

72. COMMUNITY

Only by creating cyberspace in which meaningful emotional relationships are formed with the environments in which we ourselves find meaningful presence, will we be able to design alternate realities where others might thrive and find architecturally rewarding (Borre Ludvigsen).

In *Commonspace*, Mark Surman and Darren Werschler-Henry remind us that, in cyberspace, people make the difference, not technology. They support that point with an original list of principles:

Principle 1. The collective is the Internet's killer app. The real difference between the Internet and all preceding media forms is the role it gives to people. More specifically, millions of people connected in many-to-many relationships make up communities, clans, and information gestalts, connected intelligence, the hive mind, open source, whatever you call it.
Principle 2. On-line, we're always bigger than the sum of our parts. Commonspace is a direct result of synergy. Whether they're aware of it or not people create something bigger than themselves when they connect with each other. The results can be new ideas, new products, or innovative approaches to old problems.
Principle 3. In the economy of commonspace, you need to share power to thrive. Why share power? Because connectedness makes it possible for you to benefit from and build on the success of your users and partners.
Principle 4. Mutual self-interest builds community ... and beats the corporate drones. In a many-to-many network that stresses sharing, everything that you do for yourself can benefit everyone else. Likewise, anything anyone else does can benefit you.
Principle 5. In commonspace, 15 minutes of fame is better reward than money. In many cases, the currency of commonspace is respect, small-time fame and ego boosting. Especially in technical endeavors, doing something smart and earning the respect of one's peers is of the highest order.
Principle 6. Distributed technology thrives. Siloed technology dies. Successful implementations of commonspace have to enable many-to-many relationships between people. They also need to talk to other tools using open, commonly available standards.
Principle 7. Revolution comes from the strangest places. Great new ideas in commonspace rarely come from a lab.[31]

73. Democracy

Then Dudayev said, "Russia must regret what it is doing". Borovoi's line suddenly went dead. This time, Dudayev had stayed on the phone too long (Wayne Masden, 1997).

According to Lee Miller, "cyberspace takes shape at precisely the same point where traditional definitions of public space – a physical site, a historical monument, a street or town square – fail. Architecture needs to discover how these forms fail and why these aspirations towards new virtual communities are developing". In a deep sense, cyberspace is the new public space, or "commonspace" as Mark Surman calls it. Just like the telephone, which is a universal "common carrier", the World Wide Web is the new Res Publica, the Greco-Roman notion of the common property. The global and universal accessibility of the telephone system was shown to be critical in 1989 when the Chinese government could not prevent people sending faxes abroad to tell the world about the brutal repression that greeted the Tien An Men square uprising.

Of course, cyberspace is largely occupied by private interests: at any given time, the proportion of public with respect to private space on line ("intranets" and other closed virtual networks) varies between roughly 15 and 20%. This is not really very different from the proportions between private and public space in most cities. But the key principle here is that governments and international Internet organizations protect and guarantee the conditions of access and use to all people, that is by keeping standards, codes and protocols universal in their basic functions leaving to individual users the liberty to fit their proprietary content in the common ground.

The principle of Democracy recognizes the connective as a new political entity, requiring a clear understanding of its rights and privileges alongside those of the collectivity and those of the private citizen. It is founded on the new response-ability exercised by anybody on-line.

74. Autonomy

A critical issue that concerns the democratic principle of the Res Publica is that it exists not only to provide citizens with a common ground, but also to guarantee their rights to the "res privata", the right to privacy and civil liberties. Likewise, there is a need to use the power of the code to guarantee privacy and freedom of action to all netizens. The problem is complicated, as we have seen in chapter 2, by the fact that networks are on the way to becoming ubiquitous, really inescapable once they go wireless and they establish necessary mutual positioning and defining connections. Public administrators may be tempted to both control and monitor access and activities among different groups, especially among powerful governments such as those of the US or France. The Electronic Frontier Foundation was created precisely to help guarantee civil liberties in cyberspace.

The choice, however, is not merely political; it is more profoundly sociological and psychological. Indeed, the Res Publica was a sociopolitical consequence of the split of psychological space into the subjective, private mental space, and the objective, public or social space. The rules devised in one guaranteed the continuity of the other. The same goes for our present situation: one of the key issues to be resolved in the next few years in all the successful democracies of the planet will be to decide if the constitution of the private, individual person remains both a viable entity within the networked society and thus, at least in principle, inviolable. This is particularly urgent at a time when the US congress, purportedly to protect people in case of emergencies, is examining the right of the state to keep track of every citizen who carries a cellular phone. This kind of surveillance potential cost his life to the chief of the Chechen rebels when the Russian artillery trained a rocket on Dzokhar Dudayev's position thanks to the coordinates revealed by his cell phone.

> Just seconds before what were to be the Chechen's last words, a Russian Sukhoi Su-25 jet, armed with air-to-surface missiles, had received his coordinates. It locked on to Dudayev's phone signal and fired two laser-guided missiles. (Wayne Masden, 1997).

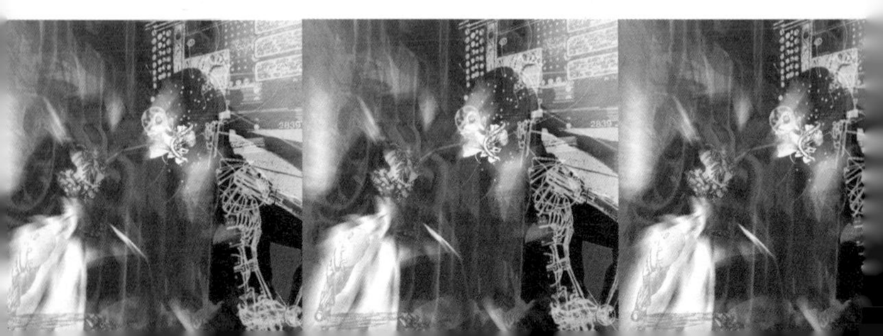

75. Ubiquity

Ubiquity is clearly not least among the main principles. If I put it last, it is because ubiquity is what is new and specific about the virtual in networks. Networks spell the elimination of distance, which is resulting now in a kind of implosion or collapsing of the planet on the single person, whether literally as in the case of "global actors" such as Bill Gates or Osama Ben Ladin, or figuratively as in "wherever I am with my palmtop and my cellphone, there is the world". Ubiquitous and mutual access to and from also brings validity to a momentous change of scale taking place right now, as a new globality is setting in not merely on the economic level, but principally at the psychological level.

We are well into the momentum of continentalization that Orwell predicted in 1984, but not as darkly. Satellites communication systems have initiated the continentalization not only of Europe but also of North and South America (Mercosur) and the Pacific area. What satellites do is that they unify the geopolitical areas of their footprints, not only from an economical standpoint, but also psychological. We see our continent every evening on the TV weather report, and that ritual keeps us in the semi-conscious awareness of our neighbors, as well as expanding our internal psychological scope.

However, for many people, globalization is a dirty word. They resist it quite naturally when all it evokes is more power to the powerful. As if seeming to favor only the people in power, the Internet is often accused of deepening the great divide between the haves and the have-nots. But it is quite the opposite on both counts: first it empowers anybody, not just the powerful among those who gain access to it, in ways that were never available before. The Internet allowed the organization of meetings such as those of Seattle at the WTO and of Porto Alegre. Second, by implication, it invites even those members of different cultures and societies who do not have direct access, to share, at least by proxy, in the international discourse.

We are now in a transition period where, as Le Corbusier did in 1924, we need to rethink not just the city, but the whole world. One of our primary concerns should be to find strategies to include a sense of the global within the local community. There is some urgency to this as the global strife is imploding upon everyone and connected architecture can do something about it. The cybertectural extension of the built environment allows cybertects to consider truly global architecture for the first time in human history.

76. Globalism

The Internet has brought about a virtual stateless zone between nations (Tajima Noriyuki, 1998).

The aim is to bring globalism to the Earth, the way civism developed in cities. This is not an overnight affair, but it is clear that architecture has a role to play in it just as it did to make cities safe and livable. But, in order to match the significance of civism, the meaning of "globalism" has to be refined. For example the "global" is not one big mass of uniform territory:

> The way in which people use networks is strongly determined by the local contexts in which they live, so that, as a social and cultural space, the electronic networks are not so much a global but a translocal structure, which connects many local situations and creates a heterogeneous translocal stratum, rather than a homogeneous global stratum (KRF, p. 198).

More specifically, "translocal architecture" wants to be clearly associated with connecting buildings and public areas which evidence common purposes on a global scale. There is a Japanese-American organization called GreenSpace which is thinking along those lines:

> The purpose of the GreenSpace program is to develop and demonstrate a new global communications and information environment for the twenty-first century. We envision sensory-rich, highly interactive, virtual environments (GreenSpaces) that can link human senses and minds across the world. We believe a new communications medium of this type will: 1) help the peoples of the world transcend geographic, language and cultural differences; 2) facilitate global collaboration to solve pervasive problems and realize untapped economic opportunities; and 3) make communication more efficient and conserve energy resources by moving our minds and information around the world at the speed of light, instead of moving mass (paper, ourselves and so on).[32]

The virtual Green and other GreenSpace projects tend to favor high-tech solutions and predominantly cyberspatial applications of VR to increase the sensory components of telepresence.

77. Simultaneity / Real / Timeliness

The global city is not a place, but a process (Manuel Castells, 1996).

There may be more democratic and equally effective possibilities immediately at hand. I have been dreaming for years about two projects, which could be realized with minimum technical investment for maximum social return: *The Global Village Square* and *The European Place*.

The Global Village Square (GVS)
Consider a public but covered area in the city or town where you live. In Toronto, I imagine that the Eaton Mall or Calatrava's magnificent BCE place would serve the purpose, but a better example might be the Galleria next to the Duomo in Milano. It would be relatively easy and comparatively inexpensive for Telecom Italia and Bell Canada to install half a dozen large video screens or more depending on the available wall area, preferably out of reach to protect them against vandalism. On each screen, a videoconferencing signal would bring a real-time image from other GVS elsewhere in the world, say the Red Square in Moscow, Times Square in New York, Tien An Men in Beijing and place des Vosges in Paris. Ideally there would be a network of these GVSs all over the world, wherever the local telecommunication companies would be willing to provide the communication for free. This would be a concept like the Virtual Green, but much closer to their original idea, which is to emulate the facilities of parks and greens.

When they arrive in the area designated for the connection, people must be able not only to see each other in proportions similar to how they would see each other in a common town square, but also to hear the sounds coming from the other side in spite of the noisy context of a shopping center. Indeed, each side could be enabled to hear the sounds coming from the other side, including conversations, thanks to a sound-focusing device invented at MIT's Media Lab. This is a kind of sound-gun that can project and locate at a specific area against a noisy background whatever sound source is taken for the projection. I can easily imagine a kind of cupola where people could gather on both sides to speak to each other.

78. Trans-localism

What I see is a permanent window opened between two cities across the ocean. It is critical that even if, on the surface, it entails higher costs, the space thus created be opened permanently, night and day. This structure is not to be time-based on punctual events, but the establishment of a real space. People at a great distance will eventually come to feel that they share a common space, just as they can share the public space of a park.

The Global Village Square (GVS) is grounded in electronic, not physical space, but it is just as durable and at least as "natural" as electric lighting in the city. The space joining Milano and Toronto, for example, would be the first of its kind in history, but I expect that one day many cities, including some of the economically and politically struggling communities will be connected this way. This kind of development may one day be required to install and maintain peace and global civility. To my mind, the GVS fulfills all the objectives proposed by GreenSpace and more precisely because it is an entirely open and public proposition. The significant socializing effect would be to include countries and people that, for political, economic and social reasons may not yet feel part of the global discourse. I see this kind of project as a healing strategy for countries such as Serbia or East Timor where advanced nations have recently obtained a better access and where the local infrastructure could be made to support it.

The European Place
As an ex-European and a very frequent traveler to the many countries of Europe, I am always amazed at their profound – and exciting – social and cultural differences and at the fact that the dream of the European community is still standing in spite of them. I am surprised at the ready acceptance of the Euro, which is about to wipe out one of the mainstays of national identities, their local currencies. Apart from the new level of taxes each member country has to pay to stay member, the sole unifying symbol for the European community is the blue flag with golden stars, admittedly a good design item, but not really a very convincing international rallying symbol.

79. Public Domain

The concept of the *European Place* is simple: in each city, town and even village within the European community, a real town square or formal place would be selected and named the *European Place* (or plaza, or square or piazza, depending on the language spoken locally). This selection would, of course be done by local authorities in democratic consultation with the local electorate. The task of the local municipal authority would be to ensure that in the chosen place a free access to networked communications be made available to the public. An existing building, say the town hall, a public library, a school, a post office or even a local café would be designated as the "European Community Access Point" and clearly marked as such. The place itself would keep its original name but the nameplate would carry the colors of Europe, the golden stars on the blue background.

The objective is to create everywhere in Europe a greater sense of the European unity within its essential diversity. A secondary objective is to encourage access and routine use of networked communications in every nook and cranny of the European community. The concept of the European Place combines the real and the virtual to support political and social cohesion over a large and diverse territory.

It would be ideal, but of course unlikely, that access to the network be provided free of charge at the local access point. Whatever the financial implications, the connection would always lead automatically to the European Community portal, a site common to all access points and available in all the languages spoken in Europe. This portal would be open to services pertaining both to local and continental information. The local information would be provided locally and be accessible from any access point, but the European information and services, including news about the EC and manpower needs in various localities, would be the responsibility of the EC. The need for high level connected architecture as well as top quality design would be evident at the EC level.

80. Changing Scale

The idea behind the *European Place* is that it should reinforce the sense of belonging not only to one's country of origin, but also to the larger context of Europe. Besides having access to connectivity, a Dutch, German or Italian person in Spain or France would "feel different" in a town square that was dedicated to Europe.

A related project that could be inserted in the context and the infrastructure of the *European Place* would be to constitute a "European Public Domain" database of all the literature, arts and cultural artifacts that are digitizable and thus made accessible on line. This database would be accessible free of charge as a common European Heritage and the contents could be reused in different combinations by the world's cybernauts.

The projects above reflect many of the principles invoked in this book and all of the ones invoked in this chapter. However they reflect more specifically five principles that I consider especially pertinent to connected architecture that are Connectivity, Ubiquity, Materiality, Democracy and Community.

No place is totally remote to anybody anymore. We are beginning to feel concerned just as much about the oppression of women in Afghanistan or the plight of East Timor, or child labor in the sweatshops of developing countries, or the rebuilding of Serbia and Kosovo as we do about the poor in the streets back home. Furthermore the necessity to promote network development and include the underprivileged is henceforth taken more seriously even by the powers that be. Global representation is now being mounted on both sides. In 2001, there were over twice as many attendants at the "Anti-Davos" meeting of non-governmental organizations in Porto Allegre, Brazil, as at the famous World Economic Forum in Switzerland. The new context is not the nation, but the globe.

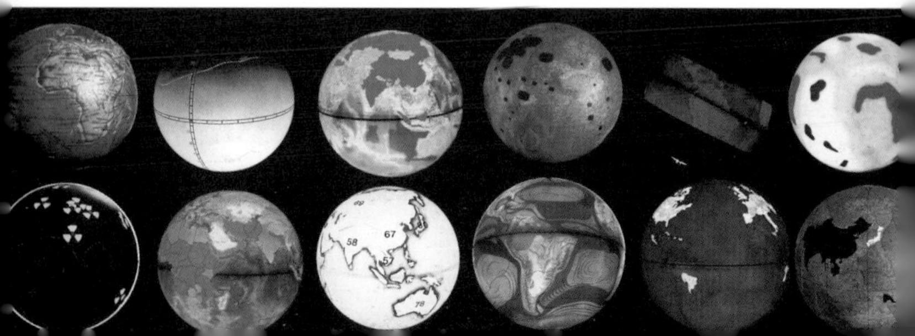

81. Knowing Desire

I think the question we must face at this moment in our history is that of our desires and whether or not we want to be responsible for our desires (Humberto Maturana, *Metadesign*, vol. 2, p. 171)

While this change of scale could be experienced even by people living in remote parts of Africa, India and China, it is not yet made conscious. International organizations and goodwill societies as well as the fast increasing number of non-governmental organizations do the best they can, but for the common people, they remain abstract. Even as they address more pressing needs than being wired, they are perceived as help coming from an unknown world. What needs to happen is not simply to "wire all nations", but also to invite people to feel part of the world and not relegated to their local scene. What is needed is a set of global, instant, permanent, translinguistic and immediately usable and empowering transcultural and translocal metaphors. That is where a change of scale in architectural and cybertectural concepts is called for. Of all the means by which cultural artifacts and media could spread the necessary perception of the equality of all inhabitants of the Earth, I believe that connected architecture and global architecture in particular would be the most effective in the short and the long run.

> Certainly I know much of what is said and is happening in the domain of globalization of the flow of information, but it is not information that constitutes the reality that we live. This reality arises instant after instant through the configuration of emotions that we live, and which we conserve with our living instant after instant. But if we know this, if we know that the reality that we live arises through our emotioning, and we know that we know, we shall be able to act according to our awareness of our liking or not liking the reality that we are bringing forth with our living. That is, we shall become responsible for what we do (Humberto Maturana).

Inhabiting Media

The grid and the network. The alphabet and the Internet. Two technologies of the mind, two forms of space. Two structures, two frames, two very different tools to watch, understand and create the world around us. A basic concept is presented here, the concept of the tie between technology and thought, mind and space. In fact, if it is legitimate to believe that the use of the Greco-Latin alphabet, emphasizing the analytical ability of the mind, may have induced an objective analytical attitude toward space, thus transforming perception (from something substantially not separated from the body to something external, the object of attitude and measurement), then it is also legitimate and necessary to ask one's self if and how the new tools of information processing are transforming our mind and our perception of the world.
From this point of view it would seem possible that if the effect of an analytical, or *alphabetical*, attitude toward space has brought about a division between the subjective dimension of man as a thinking being (and therefore a carrier of his own mental theater) and the objective dimension of a collective scenario in which individual actions take place, the effect of that which we could call a *connective*, or medial, attitude seems to stimulate a new concept of space as an active field of interactions. A new continuity, or *electromagnetic webness* between subjects that are spatially distant and qualitatively different such as bodies, things and the overall whole, the constructed environment that surrounds us. But more precisely, in what way can the new network architecture (or rather the presence and diffusion of the Internet and distributed information technology) stimulate not only a new idea of space but also a concrete revival of the architectural project?
The thoughts of Derrick de Kerckhove show us a way to attempt to answer this question. The *architecture of the network* (i.e. the deep structure of the new webness) seems to have three fundamental characteristics: that of being a mixed architecture, i.e. of having a base or real infrastructure from which a virtual extension emerges; that of being an interfaced architecture, i.e. of being an active organizational device of input and output flows; and that of being an architecture of interconnections, i.e. a spatial system whose main objective is not statically storing contents but acting as a system of interchange, or connection, between here and elsewhere, individual and collective, in a networked total surround system that overturns the distance, frontal perspective and unidirectional quality of the prospective grid.
In consideration of this: is it possible to imagine attributing to our spaces a new virtual extension, a new interface quality to the walls, and a new dynamic or interactive capacity to the inclusive and static dimension of constructions?
Rather than seeking a vague, theoretical response, let us try to understand how design research is trying to answer this question through several concrete examples where it is possible to recognize a consideration or an effective attempt at applying one of the above mentioned "principles": architecture as infrastructure, as interface, as a system of interconnection.
Therefore, architecture as infrastructure or as a material device to access the immaterial, as a system for moving material/information: an almost literal transposition of this possibility in constructed space is proposed and subsequently substantially realized by Rem Koolhaas, first in the design for the Art and Technology Center in Karlsruhe and later in a private home in Bordeaux. The design for what the architect would define as Electronic Bauhaus planned for a large box-like structure characterized by the presence of a mobile space, called *robot*. The robot, running across the building, would have worked as an electronic server bringing from one floor to the

next the technical equipment necessary for installations and performances. If the Bauhaus of Gropius dominated the carriage road that ran alongside it, absorbing it in turn into its mechanical space, the Bauhaus of Koolhaas incarnates or visceralizes the idea of an electronic infrastructure that architecture distributes in space.
The project stayed on the drawing board but the idea returned and was made concrete in the construction of a private home whose owner was paralyzed and forced into a wheelchair following an accident. In this case, the heart of the dwelling became a mobile platform that crossed and vertically joined the three floors of the house, giving access to all possible (physical!) information, gathered in transparent shelving running around the three floors of the house. Books, art objects and bottles of wine represent the virtual space that this platform/search engine can bring. Obviously, this is a metaphorical transposition of the problem but the house was definitely born out of the intention and desire to find a form of connection between constructed space and information space and the suggested path is that of architecture as a new infrastructure, a technological device that allows us access to the virtual but also, and above all, to give access to the virtual from inside the real.
Furthermore, if the approach of Koolhaas to the new society of bits is still substantially conceptual and metaphorical, it is precisely the young Dutch groups who are clarifying the issue of how to transform this new and powerful material, the bit, into architectural material.
In particular, in the work of Van Berkel and Caroline Bos (UN Studio), Kas Oosterhuis (Oosterhuisassociates), and Lars Spuybroek (Nox), the problem of the reciprocal integration between *form* and *information*, or between static objects and dynamic data flows, has become the central issue in some surprising design experiments. Many lines of research have sprung from one common initial question. So, if the attention of Van Berkel is prevalently aimed at the study of public space (to which he attempts to attribute a more and more open and flexible configuration, extrapolating from the analysis of mobility or movement flows of the urban area in question, see for example the project for the Arnhem Centre Infrastructure), for Oosterhuis and Spuybroek the central question to be resolved is that of the relationship between *human body* and *constructed body*. But if for Oosterhuis the body is essentially a living system that could suggest to architecture new models of interactivity (based on the possibility of attributing a programmable *electronic skin* to the constructed, characterized by dynamic and multimedia "contents", symbolic of the *transPORTs 2001* project), for Spuybroek the body is fundamentally a system in movement, a movement that can be amplified or disturbed through an architectural system conceived as a prosthetic extension of the body itself (and thus as a wheel, a skate, a car, an *object-vector* not limited to passively housing the body but one that actively accompanies the movement, consider the dynamic and interactive nature of the *fresh H2O Pavilion*).
It is interesting to note that, in this research, it is evident that the central node of a possible metamorphosis of architecture no longer regards either any particularly imaginative ability, in the distribution and division of environments, or any particular technical/tectonic daring in experimenting with continually more extreme balances and configurations. In fact, the legendary challenge to gravity seems to have been replaced by a much less evident challenge though more complex, a challenge that is played out mainly *on the surface*. In other words, in the possibility of rethinking the limit as something that is extremely flexible and deformable, or as a chance for *unfolding* rather than containing, as a center of action rather than a periphery of movement: in the apparent bi-dimensionality of the surface, a surprising possibility of growth of space seems in fact to be nested.

The reconfiguration of the architectural surface as a sensitive, flexible and interactive membrane represents a real revolution of the constructed world, founded for millennia on the indisputable concept of stability. The interface is the opposite of stability. It is a system of dialogue, of intermediation, of passage, of exchange. Attributing to constructed architecture this ability for dialogue means being uprooted from the stability of matter, recalling that matter is energy, searching for a new convergence between matter and information.
An extremely interesting approach to the possibility of experimenting with a new intermediate state of matter between the solid and liquid characterizes the most recent experiments by Marcos Novak, aimed at exploring the idea of a *subversion* of the real by the virtual. Beginning with the observation that a great part, or more precisely most, of reality is invisible to our senses, the problem of a possible extension/transformation of the territory of architecture certainly has to do with giving the *invisible* the possibility of manifesting itself, operating at the margins of dissolution and exceeding the limits of manifested aspects and the potential quality of the space.
A project born out of the collaboration between Novak and Oosterhuis with the precise objective of concretely experimenting with the possibility of interconnection between virtual space and real space is *TransPorts 2001*, a "game of evolution" in real time played between a certain number of port cities and a website.
The connection between the pavilions in the various cities and the network is created via cameras whose shots are reciprocally exchanged between one pavilion and another and recomposed or unified in the virtual pavilion on the Internet. The visitors, both physical and virtual, to the pavilion are the players/navigators of a real/virtual space in which these produce changes in shape, color and *content*. In fact, the internal covering of the pavilion is a flexible electronic skin capable of visualizing texts and images in real time. So while the physical visitor acts with their own movement, or their own physical presence on the sensor-field that characterizes the interior space of the real pavilion, the virtual visitor can input any type of data so that it is presented inside the space, a space that thus becomes a complex vehicle of communication where the real and the virtual are intimately connected and free to act on each other. In summary, the physical pavilion is a structure that can be manipulated in real time from a website that in turn is modified by whatever happens in the real space. The informational input is combined with local factors. The network navigation is mixed with the navigation of real space transformed into an interactive field of sensors and switches.
What might be worth mentioning is that the network has already substituted the grid. Our bodies are already constantly *immersed* in a continuous space, sensitive and interactive, where, in every part of the planet, access is possible to an infinite universe of information, of connections, of people on-line perhaps on the other side of the globe.
If, as McLuhan rightly understood, one of the most important phenomena of the electronic era consisted in creating a global network, or a unified field of experience, today the possibility of understanding the fundamental characteristics of this new networked condition, or *webness* like de Kerckhove says, is the first indispensable step in understanding how to produce a new architecture, i.e. an architecture intimately connected to the electronic era in which we live.

MARIALUISA PALUMBO
malupa@libero.it

Notes

CHAPTER 1

1. Margaret Wertheim, *The Pearly Gates of Cyberspace: A History of Space from Dante to the Internet*, W.W. Norton & Company, 1999, p. 219.

2. Michael Benedikt, *Cyberspace: First Steps*, The MIT Press, Cambridge 1991, p. 124.

3. Anna Cicognani (1998), *On the Linguistic Nature of Cyberspace and Virtual Communities*, Springer-Verlag, London, vol. 3: 16–24, pp. 17–18. G.A. Kelly, *The Psychology of Personal Constructs*, Norton, New York 1955. Id., *A Brief Introduction to Personal Construct Theory*, Bannister, D., ed., Perspectives in Personal Construct Theory, Academic Press, London, p. 1-29.

4. Borre Ludvigsen, *Presence and Form in the Architecture of Cyberspace*. This paper is available at *http://www.architexturez.com*.

5. Roy Ascott, *The Architecture of Cyberception. Leonardo Electronic Almanac*, 2 (8), *http://www-mitpress.mit.edu/LEA/home.html*. Also in M. Toy (ed.), *Architects in Cyberspace*, Academy Editions, London 1994, pp. 38-41. This paper is available at *http://www.ma.ca/book*.

6. Anna Cicognani, *Architectural Design for Online Environments*, paper posted on the Web at *http://www.arch.usyd.edu.au/~anna/*.

CHAPTER 2

7. M. Wertheim, *op.cit.*, p. 229.

8. Wade Rowland, *The Spirit of the Web*, Somerville Press, Toronto 1994, p. 45.

9. Erik Davis, *Techgnosis: Myth, Magic + Mysticism in the Age of Information*, Harmony Books, New York 1998.

10. Karsten Harries, *The Ethical Function of Architecture*, The MIT Press, Cambridge 1998.

11. Lawrence Lessig, *Code and other Laws of Cyberspace*, Basic Books, 1999, p. 89.

12. *Ibid.*, p.35.

CHAPTER 3

13. Roy Ascott, *op. cit.*, p. 38.

14. From an interview with Doug Engelbart quoted in Bob Cotton and Richard Oliver, *Understanding Hypermedia 2000*, 2nd ed., Phaidon Press, London 1997, p. 31.

15. George Landow, *Hypertext 2.0: The Convergence of Contemporary Critical Theory and Technology(Parallax - Re-Visions of Culture and Society)*, 2nd ed. Johns Hopkins University Press, 1997.

16. Tim Berners-Lee, *The World Wide Web: A very short personal history*. Go to *http://www.w3.org/People/Berners-Lee/ShortHistory.html*. Martin Dodge and Rob Kitchin, *Mapping Cyberspace*, Routledge, London 2001.

17. Steve Aukstakalnis and David Blattner, *Silicon Mirage: The Art and Science of Virtual Reality*, Peachpit Press, Berkeley 1992.

18. Jennny Holzer, *Architectural Design, VR: An Emerging Medium*, Academy Edition, London 1994, p.9.

19. William Mitchell, *E-Topia: Urban Life, Jim - But Not As We Know It*, The MIT Press, Cambridge 1999, p. 60.

CHAPTER 4
20. To know more about Disalvo, go to his handsome site: *http://www.walkerart.org/salons/shockoftheview/space/disalvo/space.html.*
21. Tanaka Jun and Tajima Noriyuki, "Cyberspace and the City / Architecture/ the Body", in *Intercommunication*, 24, Spring 1998, pp.74-85.
22. Bernd Meurer, *The Future of Space*, Campus Pub, 1994, p. 199.
23. Neal Stephenson, *Snow Crash*, 1992. pp. 24-25.
24. Reinhard W. Wolf, *Digital Cities in the Data Network – from Metaphor to Reality*, in Soke Dinkla (ed.), *Connected Cities: Processes Of Art In The Urban Network*, 1998, p. 87.
25. For papers by Ludvigsen, go to *http://www.ludvigsen.hiof.no/webdoc/mediaseminar/ai.html.*
26. For a large selection of spectacular images, go to *http://129.102.224.90/vretina/images/.*

CHAPTER 5
27. *Ibid.*, p. 84
28. William Mitchell , *op. cit.*, pp. 147–154.
29. Thomas Horan, *Digital Places: Building Our City of Bits*, The Urban Land Institute, 2000.
30. All quotes including the tables are from Anna Cicognani's, *Architectural Design for Online Environments*, in press, 2000. The draft of this paper can be found at: *www.arch.usyd.edu.au/~anna.*
31. Raymond, Eric, *The Cathedral and the Bazaar, www.tuxedo.org/~esr/writings/cathedral-bazaar/cathedral-bazaar/.*
32. Mark Surman and Darren Werschler-Henry, *CommonSpace: The Business of Building e-Community*, 2000.
33. Paper presented at IEEE Proceedings of the Networked Reality Workshop, October 26-28, 1995, Boston, MA.

Credits

P. 7: *Tokyo city grid*, public domain. P. 8: *Contextuality*, Tonik Wojtyra. P. 9: *Perspecitivism*, Tonik Wojtyra. P. 10: *Symmetry*, Peter Marshall. P. 11: *VisualBias*, Marc Ngui. P. 12: *Mental space 1*, Marc Ngui. P. 13: *Mental space 2*, Marc Ngui. P. 14: *Perspecitivism*, Tonik Wojtyra. P. 15: *Connectivity 2*, Marc Ngui. P. 16: *Quantum Thinking*, Marc Ngui. P. 17: *Little Big/Small*, Peter Anders. P. 18-19: *Cybertecture*, Marc Ngui. P. 20-21: *Muscle plug*, collage by PeterMarshall. P. 22: *Complexity*, Tonik Woytira. P. 24: *Warriors of the Net*, © 99 Gunilla Elam, Ericsson Medialab. P. 27: *Complexity*, Tonik Woytira. P. 28: *Cyberception 1, 2, 3*, collage by Peter Marshall. P. 29-30: *Codicity*, Tonik Wojtyra. P. 31: *Riding theCode*, Marc Ngui. P. 32: *Nodes Modes Codes*, Marc Ngui. P. 33: image by Peter Marshall. P. 34: image by Peter Marshall. P. 35: *Electrification of language*, Peter Marshall. P. 36: *Mind Dive*, Marc Ngui. P. 37: *Crowds*, Marc Ngui. P. 38: image by Peter Marshall. P. 39: *Sharing*, Marc Ngui. P. 40: *Hypercube*, Maurice Benayoun. P. 41: *First Design for the Web*, Tim Berners-Lee. P. 42: *Planet Multicast* is a visualisation of the global topology of the Internet MBone. The MBone is the Internet's multicast backbone. Multicast is the most efficient way of distributing data from one sender to multiple receivers with minimal packet duplication, Tamara Munzner. P. 43: *Map of the Market*, from SmartMoney.com, maps the stock performance of US corporations. Individual companies are represented by different plots of land sized according to their market capitalisation. The colour of the plot indicates recent changes in stock price, SmartMoney.com. P. 44: *Starrynight* is an interface artwork by Alex Galloway and Mark Tribe. All texts in *Starrynight* were written by members of the Rhizome community, Mark Tribe *mark@rhizome.org*; Alex Galloway *alex@rhizome.or*. Martin Wattenberg *w@bewitched.com*. Java programming was provided by Martin Wattenberg. Editorial assistance was provided by Rachel Greene. Design assistance was provided by Chris Graves. P. 45: *The Long View*, Marc Ngui. P. 46: *Feedback*, Marc Ngui. P. 47: *Tactility Image*, Arnold Wu. P. 48: *Crossing Talks*, Maurice Benayoun. P. 49: *Screen*, Marc Nguiv. P. 50: *Galeria Virtual*, Roc and Narcís Parés. P. 51: *Tunnel Paris New Delhi*, Maurice Benayoun. P. 52: *Osmose*, Char Davies. P. 53: Nox, *Lars Spuybroek OfftheRoad_5 speed*, prefabricated housing near Eindhoven, Netherlands. P. 54: Stepen Perrella, digital model of the *Möbius House* and project for the *Haptic Horizon*. P. 55: Marcos Novak, *Paracube* project. P. 56: *Electronic Café*, Kit Galloway and Sherrie Rabinowitz. P. 57: ag4 mediatecture company, *Start Amadeus*. P. 58: ag4 mediatecture company, *Start Amadeus*. P. 59: Tate Gallery's web site. P. 60: *The Invisible Shape of Things Past*, Art + Com. P. 61: Jean-Philippe Durrios, *Virtual Worlds*. P. 62: Images of the winning design entry for *The U* in Sherwood Towne, Alpha World, Designed by Hentik G, Zg & Aurac (Active Art Design) for an Activeworlds competition P. 63: *The Growth of Alphaworld*, Alphaworlds. P. 64: *Netzspannung*, Monika Fleischmann and Wolfgang Strauss. P. 65: *Interactive Plant Growing*, Christa Sommerer. P. 66: *Networked Skin*, Christian Moeller. P. 67: Monolab's work's. P. 68: *Alzado Vectorial*, Rafael Lozano-Hemmer. P. 69: *Art Impact – collective retinal memory*, Maurice Benayoun. P. 71: Ortlos Architects, *City at Once* (left), *Library for the Information Age* (right). P. 72: *Miniaturisation/digitisation*, collage by Galit Szolomowicz. P. 73: *Crossing Talks*, Maurice Benayoun. P. 74: *Touch Knowledge*, Marc Ngui. P. 75: *Phantom Screens*, Peter Marshall. P. 76: *Point of Being*, Marc Ngui. P. 77: image by Marc Ngui P. 78: *Soft Hills*, Marc Ngui. P. 79: The Wall on Treptower Strasse in the district of Neukolln, 1983. Photographs by Harry Hempel from the book *Wo die Mauer war?* (*Where was the Berlin Wall?*), Nicolai, Belin 1999. Treptower Strasse at the corner of Heidelbergstrasse, 1994, Photographs by Harry Hempel, *ibid*. P. 80: *Machine Kiss*, Peter Marshall. P. 82: *Sharing*, Marc Ngui. P. 83: *Art Impact – collective retinal Memory*, Maurice Benayoun. P. 84-85: *European Place*, Arnold Wu. P. 86-87: *World Processor*, Ingo Gunther.

The IT Revolution in Architecture
Series edited by **Antonino Saggio**

The Information Technology Revolution in Architecture is a new series reflecting on the effects the virtual dimension is having on architects and architecture in general. Each volume will examine a single topic, highlighting the essential aspects and exploring their relevance for the architects of today.

Other titles in this series:

Information Architecture
Basis and future of CAAD
Gerhard Schmitt
ISBN 3-7643-6092-5

HyperArchitecture
Spaces in the Electronic Age
Luigi Prestinenza Puglisi
ISBN 3-7643-6093-3

Digital Eisenman
An Office of the Electronic Era
Luca Galofaro
ISBN 3-7643-6094-1

Digital Stories
The Poetics of Communication
Maia Engeli
ISBN 3-7643-6175-1

Virtual Terragni
CAAD in Historical and Critical Research
Mirko Galli / Claudia Mühlhoff
ISBN 3-7643-6174-3

Natural Born CAADesigners
Young American Architects
Christian Pongratz / Maria Rita Perbellini
ISBN 3-7643-6246-4

New Wombs
Electronic Bodies and Architectural Disorders
Maria Luisa Palumbo
ISBN 3-7643-6294-4

New Flatness
Surface Tension in Digital Architecture
Alicia Imperiale
ISBN 3-7643-6295-2

Digital Design
New Frontiers for the Objects
Paolo Martegani / Riccardo Montenegro
ISBN 3-7643-6296-0

Aesthetics of Total Serialism
Contemporary Research from Music to Architecture
Markus Bandur
ISBN 3-7643-6449-1

Advanced Technologies
Building in the Computer Age
Valerio Travi
ISBN 3-7643-6450-5

For our free catalog please contact:

Birkhäuser – Publishers for Architecture
P. O. Box 133, CH-4010 Basel, Switzerland
Tel. ++41-(0)61-205 07 07; Fax ++41-(0)61-205 07 92
e-mail: sales@birkhauser.ch
http://www.birkhauser.ch